The 3-Step
Digital Detox
System

81 Solutions to Beat Technology Addiction and Reduce Screen Time

Increase Your Productivity and Take Back Control in a World Full of Distractions

NEIL KRISTOFF COOPER

Table of Contents

Introduction

*T*he thud of hitting the dirt knocked the wind out of me. For a moment, all I could hear was a shrieking whistle in my ears, but then everything went silent as the thudding of my head died down.

I looked down at my scraped hands: thick layers of dirt stuck to the small bleeding slots within them. At first, I had no idea what had happened. One minute I was slicing through the wind like a superhero, winning the battle of staying on the platform. Then, before I knew it, I was holding on for dear life, which was less daunting but necessary because, within a split second, I got thrown into a cloud of dust. Now, here I was: On the ground.

With a groan, I lifted my body like a beached walrus to glare at the roundabout as it swung around. What a treacherous varmint! Someone has to stop it—it cannot prevail!

I looked around the playground but found no sign of anyone, only a few pigeons plucking the soil. A deep frown cracked on my forehead, and tears threatened to spill. I pulled myself up from the ground, standing firmly in place, assertive, and determined to hide my weaknesses and frailties. I cannot let it win…No, let me rephrase that: I will not allow it to win, and today it was up to me alone to defeat my foe.

Blood was gushing from the cuts on my knees and trickling down my shins. It burns. However, I guess my adrenaline and heroism will keep me going through the pains—they have to.

Within a millisecond of a moment, after gathering up all of my courage, my hands balled up into fists, and I charged at full speed toward the rotating disk. I grinned, daring my enemy to compete. The villain goes down today! I will not be defeated by something as simple as a roundabout. No, not a chance!

It is fair to say that it was already late when my mother called for me. I regretted my decision to take on the playground ride again, especially when I had to wash up later that night, and I could feel every bruise and abrasion my adventure had given me. It was awful. However, even when it was all fun, games, and regrets, I would not have swapped these memories for anything in the world. The pain, it seems, goes hand in hand with being a child.

It seems that I am a bit homesick and nostalgic for less complicated times when things were simpler and there were no cables beside my bed, grounding me to them.

It is almost as if the internet and the world of technology have become a significant part of who we are now and how we strike down the hours. The thought of the roundabout came to me when I saw a little kid playing on a tablet. I could not help but wonder where the times of getting hurt and playing outside had gone, or was it just me getting old? Those were memorable days, and that is a claim I simply cannot fabricate. It was great.

I am not throwing shade at parents who hand their tablets or other devices to their children for them to explore and play on. No, not at all;

it most definitely is not my place. I am just thinking to myself and out loud about the good times when all I wanted was to play, get dirty, and unintentionally beat myself up. While now, I am here in a world where I barely get the time to get away from the screens and unwind without the digital world knocking at the front door.

I think you and I are in the same boat and that you can, to some degree, relate to what I am saying or at least trying to state. Do you often find your attention being tugged and pulled at all sides, and you have, ultimately, lost control over that one thing that had made your life your own?

Whether it is from the tone of your text messages, the dings from social media, or the ringing of your email notifications, you often find yourself distracted—misplaced within a world you cannot touch.

Even when you know that your habits are detrimental to your daily life and that, deep down, something has to be done, you often find yourself back in the same spot, surrounded by buttons and a search bar.

Times come along when you feel helpless, confused, and let down. I get it; I really do. So, what would you say if I were to tell you that with the right set of tools and strategies, you can have control back over the life you so deeply desire? Well, get your speech and trainers in place because that is precisely what I am telling you.

In this book, I will share with you the three steps of taking up a digital detox system that can help you grab the reins and autonomy in your life that has long been driven by the digital world.

You will find not only the science behind the theories but ways and practical advice that you can readily apply to your daily routines. These can help you develop a healthier and sustainable digital lifestyle where you master your tech and internet use and lessen the power it has to distract and grip its hold on you. If we are honest, it is where you finally get that couples counseling you always needed to transform your relationship with technologies.

In this digital age, tech is very much a part of each of our lives. As someone who spent many years in corporate America, I know how it feels to live a life dictated by emails, internet use, and technologies. The never-ending emails filled my inbox, the internet took over my time, and I found myself glued to my devices. As a result, my feelings of anxiety, hopelessness, and fear left me bare.

I decided to put my foot down when I wasted my weekends on my devices checking emails and doing research. I then decided to learn how to better manage my digital usage by applying powerful strategies to get me back on track. As a business owner and productivity coach, I share what I have learned over the years and from the people I work with. Seeing them reclaim control over their time and attention to come up with exceptional outcomes brings tremendous satisfaction. I hope to share the same experiences and outputs with you.

The first section will drill down on the psychology that will make you better understand your addiction, as having the proper ammunition is the first step in managing your dependencies. After that, we will focus on tackling the common digital culprits in our lives and how to curb and shape them to your specifications. The last stretch we have is devoted to the strategies you can use to ensure that all your efforts do not go to waste and that they genuinely take hold and last for the long run.

As a result of the strategies outlined in this book, I was able to halt technology and the internet from running my life. Instead, I flipped over the cards and played them under my hand so that I was the one in control over how I used my gadgets and spent my time. The end goal of this all is to help you cultivate healthy behaviors that stick around and restrain your habits so that you are more productive, less absentminded, and in complete control.

Yes, addiction is no lost cause. But you can reclaim your power, and the way to do that is by weaning yourself from your tech obsessions. Patterns were made to be pulled apart and broken, and the best time to start is now.

The techniques and strategies you will read are proven to yield incredible results. Each chapter will usher you closer to your goals of living a life, goals you probably already had before the tech came and moved you. So, tell me, my reader, are you ready for a life of change?

STEP ONE:
SELF-AWARENESS LAYING THE FOUNDATIONS

Chapter 1:

What You're up Against

I know you know why you are here reading this, and you do not need me telling you why. You have already grasped your answers and reasons, after all. However, an essential part of *kicking butt, taking names*, and ultimately, getting back control over your life without the buttons means understanding and hearing it all once more. So, bear with me and these few chapters, as it will be worth it in the end.

Definition

Webster has defined addiction as "a compulsive, chronic, physiological or psychological need for a habit-forming substance, behavior, or activity having harmful physical, psychological, or social effects and typically causing well-defined symptoms (such as anxiety, irritability, tremors, or nausea) upon withdrawal," (Merriam-Webster, 1847).

This is what addiction is, whatever your vices might be: Coffee, alcohol, food, drugs, or shopping. An addiction is an addiction. In my opinion, it is anything you become dependent on and whatever makes you chase that elevated feel. It makes you feel like you are on top of the highest peak, screeching down on a slide without any apprehension and enjoying every bit of the ride! I know it is an oddly strange and specific image, but the point still stands: Whatever it is that holds you in its grip, and whatever it is you are doing, it feels incredible!

That is how it became an addiction in the first place and not something you just enjoyed doing—that chase of sensations. Then again, it is all fun and games until it is not. No matter how harmless your substance of choice might have seemed at first, it usually is not. Eventually, it just has to go; for casualty's sake.

I mean, the word addiction itself was poured from a Latin term meaning to be "enslaved by" or "bound to" (Weber, 2019). You know, which already pulls up a few red flags if you ask me. However, more often than not, we do not know we are addicted to something. Then, other times, when we know we have a problem, we simply cannot admit it out loud and to ourselves.

Addiction, even with its definition, is not effortless to wrap your head around. It is easy to understand until you are the one with your foot in the bucket. Still, no matter what your addiction looks like, they all have comparable markers and 'tells' up their sleeves which you can use to see whether or not you have some troubles to admit.

With an internet addiction, it is often shown by the extent of time you put into your tech and internet usage. You need it to feel a certain way and keep other unpleasant emotions at bay. When you do not put in that time and effort, you feel your mood change, as if you are somewhat lost without it. You cannot seem to pitch yourself away from those screens, even when neurological complications and psychological, physical, and social blows follow. Everything else swiftly and effortlessly becomes secondary, even when you cannot help yourself.

Academics, researchers, and mental health practitioners have this ongoing debate about whether or not hackneying the internet is an addiction disorder and illness on its own. Some point their fingers to other conditions, such as depression, anxiety, and other addictions. I am not at all saying they are wrong. I am a productivity coach, not a medical professional, after all. So, who am I to say otherwise?

I will say that, to some degree, I see eye to eye with this statement. Commonly, someone who develops an addiction to something has some other things picking at their core—disorders, thoughts, feelings, and traumas that lack addressing. That, yes, I understand completely.

However, I do not think internet addiction is always a symptom of another dependence, such as gambling online because of a problem with chancing your arm. Do not get me wrong—this can definitely be the case. But, sometimes, we just choose to make technology and the internet our drug of choice. Nevertheless, feel free to think and feel what you want regarding the matter. After all, we are not here to debate where internet addiction stands within the Diagnostic and Statistical Manual of Mental Disorders. We are here for a slab of self-awareness and understanding of what it is you could have, perhaps.

So, internet addiction disorder, or 'IAD,' is all about the internet and tech taking up your life. Ruling it almost to the point where it controls your day, feelings, thoughts, and other areas of your life, such as your relationships and career. It stuffs you into this clouded computer-cased bubble and leaves you to fend for yourself beneath the cables and DIMM slots.

However, this disorder has ranks falling from it, and it does not just mean chatting with people online. It mainly depends on what you are using the internet for, yes, but also that one internet activity that drives your reason for turning on that screen repeatedly. Although not limited to them, six main activities often coexist with the addiction (and yes, all were given fun names):

- Between sheets:

  This is when you use the internet for sexual content and plea-sure. It can be when you constantly look at, download, share, and swap pornographic materials or when you engage in casual cybersex with others. This may occur alongside neglecting re-al-world interactions and, sometimes, even avoiding intimate moments with your partner altogether, especially in the cases of cyber affairs.

- Making friends:

  Making friends and socializing are essential bits of life. How-ever, once you only stick to talking in chat rooms and making your friends online, your real life and surroundings can take quite the knock. You could, for example, lose your real-life companions and lock yourself away from authentic face-to-face conversations.

- Cart-pulling:

  I know I am labeling this as something to do with spending money, which it does, but there is also more to it. It can be things like gambling, trading, and shopping. Also, spending excessive time playing games. This can often lead to your wallet running short and your financial situation tumbling. While gaming could often lead to a steal in the time needed in other areas, such as your work and education, some in-game pur-chases can also cause your money to run low.

- Information overload:

    This is when you obsessively collect and search the internet for information. This can be anything from looking up new gossip about a celebrity to educational talks and blogs or even running through hours and hours of videos.

- Always online:

    Almost everyone has a social media account and profile. This is one of the highest reasons people become addicted to the internet. It could be the desire to constantly monitor what is going on. A couple good examples of platforms that facilitate this are Facebook, or Instagram, which may have you checking your DM's and posting about every single thing you do, even your whereabouts! This could also steal real-life interactions and stick you into a very narrow slip while swiping time from you and the people around you.

- Never nine-to-five:

    In recent times a lot of work has been digitalized. Now, especially with the increasing demand to work from home, it is harder for some to pull away and switch off. Some people will spend hours in front of their computers doing work and nothing else. This cycle steals a lot from relationships and removes the barrier between your personal life and career.

So, once again, these are just the common spurs people have when using the internet and tech. But they are not the only ones, and you would probably know best what stimulates and keeps you glued.

Yet, as I have said before, not all of us know what makes us so digitally dependent or whether or not we have an addiction to start. This is not something you get a *beep* about or a call telling you, "*Yes! You definitely are!"* Sometimes, when you undertake these questions and challenges alone, you will not know where to turn. But I guess that is why I am here; to guide you the best I can.

I run the risk of sounding corny and emulative saying this, but it is true. As every seminar, self-help book, and movie declared, the first step in solving a problem is admitting you have one. I do not expect you to map out an entire report on how you feel, where you fall off the wagon, your whole life story, and such. I will still help you with the basics and guidelines, of course. Or else, I would be rather pointless, wouldn't I?

However, before we get to the criteria and tell signs I have mentioned, you should understand the importance of honesty. I will list criteria from people, studies, and research notes. But, you can deem them empty if you lie to yourself when dotting the i's, crossing the t's, and seeing what boxes of the bars you fit into. You have to be open, non-judgmental, and sincere. Remember that no one is looking over your shoulder with a fault-finding gawp, or at least I hope not. Therefore, go all out and be gentle with yourself. Remember that you are not some freak of nature. This addiction is common, with over 210 million people admitting to their own internet dependencies, and that stat is over 5 years old! (Longstreet & Brooks).

With that said, I think it is about time we get down to the hard stuff and look at what might indicate you have a crisis with the internet:

- You obsess over your time on the internet, thinking about what you did the last time you were online and what you will do when you check in for your next click.

- You need to use the internet to feel cheerful and satisfied.

- In the past, you have tried to stop, control, and cut back on your internet time, but without success.

- You shift almost entirely when you are not online and experience withdrawal symptoms such as feeling restless, irritable, down in the dumps, and just overall moody.

- Whenever you do go online, you stay on longer than you intended and anticipated.

- You risk the loss of your relationships, work, education, and other opportunities, all for some screen time.

- When people ask you about your time spent on the internet, you often lie and hide the extent of time you invest.

- You use the internet as an escape route to run away from reality and all the problems, responsibilities, and feelings that come with it.

- You feel almost bare, alone, and strange without your technology. Whereas sometimes, when your phone is at home, you feel anxious to get to it.

You do not have to check out in all these areas. However, meeting at least five of them could mean taking a step back to consider how you spend your hours. Also, before it slipped my mind, this criteria was, for the most part, created by Dr. Kimberley S. Young, Keith W. Beard, and the American Psychiatric Association. So, you know that it was not thrown together by some businessman. Although I am one heck of a coach!

Furthermore, and for me, this is the one that really counts. You know who you are and why you have picked up the book. Therefore, even if you are unsure whether you meet some criteria or not, or anything like that, sit down with yourself to talk things out.

Think about whether your behavior, thoughts, and feelings change when you are without the internet. Why you use it as much, what makes you turn on the computer, and whether there are other problems you are hiding from. Really think things through and decide whether you believe you have an internet addiction truthfully.

I can give you books on what it means to have an internet issue, but at the end of the day, only you know yourself, your circumstances, and your motivations for reading this paragraph and wanting to digitally detox.

How We Got Plugged In

So, now we know all about the basics of internet addiction: What it looks like and whether you have some concerns to turn over. Next up, it is time to unveil the truth behind the addiction and how you got hooked in the first place.

I will not lie—I know exactly where you are coming from. The internet and everything you have at the edge of your fingertips is an exceptional feel and exchange. I mean, what a time to be alive! However, we all know that sometimes those things intended to be good for us, that feel just as grand, are not always best for us; and often, they do us more harm than good.

This is especially the case with the internet and how it keeps us hooked and plugged into its use and selections. There is very little information and research out there to give us an answer as to why using the internet evolves into habits and addiction.

So, let's just run with a thought for a second. Habits are behaviors, routines, and actions that come naturally. We typically do them without giving the actual act much thought. Still, we had to learn these habits by doing that single thing repeatedly until it was indented into our minds. Brushing our teeth, combing out our hair, and eating at certain times—all these daily to-dos are examples of habits we had learned when we were younger. From thereon out, we learned some more, some good ones and some we are not too fond of. If you really think about it, most of our day consists of small habits slapped together into twenty-four hours. So, I do not believe the question should be why internet use becomes a habit, but why it wouldn't become one.

When the rise of tech and the internet sprung into our lives, everything around us adapted, included, and implemented these new things and changes. Today, they have become a constant thing. We drive electric cars with screens to offices where there are computers and phones all over. Then at home, some of us have washing machines, electric toothbrushes, coffee makers, and televisions. And, believe it or not, there are more people in the world with smartphones than there are with toilets! (Zuckerman, 2020).

Technology and the internet are not these new fads that will go away soon. The fact remains that they have been around for some time, and we have constant exposure to them all. Of course, we took them in as habits of our own. The thing about habits is that some often turn sour, but that's something I do not have to tell anyone: We either eat not-so-healthy foods or possibly smoke or drink a bit more coffee than we should. There is nothing wrong with using the internet and using tech. However, this overuse leads us into this mangled mess of addiction.

Nonetheless, not all news is bad. As you would guess from the thousands of self-help books, habits are not something we are stuck with. We are free to switch and ditch them as we please. Therefore, your days of getting lost on the World Wide Web are about to be unplugged. Or, at least, that part is still to come. For now, we still have some fishing to do.

As with any addiction, there has to be something to rouse the urge. If we step back into habits, we would say that there has to be a trigger and cue so that you will actually get to the act. Then we also need that *wow* factor that makes the internet your output of choice. The internet is accessible, immediate, and interactive and hurls fields of possibilities and options. It is clear to see what charm it holds against and for us. Look, I have also used technology and the internet, so I know exactly why it is a siren for some. However, why don't we get a bit specific:

Firstly, let us look at the most obvious reasons we are so attracted to the internet and the technology we use it: It gives comfort like no other! For example, I will use three specific points of advantages of the internet: Instant gratification, data gathering, and applications.

Taking a step back a few decades, technology and the internet were new and, for many, unheard of. This was a period where some tasks required that extra stretch of effort. If you had to find specific information or dive into research, you had to pack up and hit the libraries and books. If you had to gather up some demographic data or any data about anything from products to general information, you had to move from house to house. It didn't matter that the information was very imprecise because who really opens their doors to talk about whether they like that brand of peanut butter? Not only that, but the geographical limitations alone made the data even less valuable in some scenarios.

I am sure most of us already popped into the world when computers were around, but not all of us had access to one, so the examples stay! If we compare this to how research and information gathering works today, it is easy to see how it captures you. You can simply flop open a small device, lift a metal top or push a button, and with the touch of a finger, *whoop!* You have all you need: Information, gambling opportunities, R-rated materials, lessons, and everything you can think of. While you can simply go to a word processor or online tool and create a quick survey that stretches miles, and people do not mind answering surveys as long as you do not knock on their doors.

So, in terms of instant gratification and data gathering, you got it right next to you, and we use them to make our lives easier. This brings me to applications. According to Forbes, there were 8.93 million apps in 2020 (Koetsier, 2020). Yes, that is a massive total, but it also means that software engineers and developers had over two years to create even more! You do not even want to know what kinds of apps are out there: There are pointless ones, without a doubt, and useful ones. The latter is why so many of us stuff our tech with them; to make our lives easier. It makes sense why many of us become addicted to them, but that sentence alone should tell you that it is not healthy to become so attached to them. The most addictive app out there brings me to another bait the internet brings: The interaction with others and our own fulfillment.

There are numerous chat apps and online spaces where you can communicate, connect, and share with others worldwide. This is a huge reason many of us find the internet so comforting. The way it makes us feel as if we have a giant social network of people who support us and give us a sense of community. It feels incredible when we connect with others and create meaningful relationships. Now, with the internet, you do not have to worry about whether or not you are too shy to speak. You can find others with similar interests quickly with a simple read of a bio. There is also this sense of anonymity and freedom, I think. People, for some reason, feel more unassailable to be who they are when there is a screen in front of them. You can say that, in some people, it unlocks personalities and personas they would not show in person while giving them some sense of recognition and power. This is a way of fulfilling our needs that some of us feel we cannot meet in any other way. Not all of us can be those confident, self-assured talkers that, you know, get what they want when they want. So, the internet is really an escape and open space for some.

Furthermore, a more medical and biological reason is that some people are merely more susceptible to addiction. They can have sheltered personality problems and bruises from their pasts. Perhaps, they are more addicted to those biochemical reactions of feel-good hormones from "online rewards" that just take the reins, but details will come later!

There are so many reasons, as you can see, why we get wrapped up in an addiction that steps on us and keeps us there. It is notable to understand that no one, especially me, is blaming you. These things can happen to anyone, and with this specific incentive, it is easy to get lost and tangled in the scrolls and tabs. There is nothing to be ashamed of, we all have our own things we deal with, and the internet is just one of them. You are here, and that is more than most can say. You are already bettering yourself because you want to find a way to shut down and move forward. So, I guess all that is left to say now is *kudos* to you, and see you in the next chapter!

Chapter 2:

What Keeps You Plugged

◆•————— ● —————•◆

Previously we have touched on why the internet hooks us, keeps us wanting, and all that unwanted *jazz*. Now, I want to shuffle away from that and focus on what keeps us plugged in in our lives. At the end of chapter one, I could not help myself, and I dabbled into ways we make our addiction happen. However, I also promised more details, so wait no more, as here they are.

Relationships

Relationships are essential for humans. It is genuinely something we cannot live without, or at least, we choose not to. I am also pretty sure we would go downright insane and build fruit to talk to if we were to remove human interaction altogether. That said, as important as they are, relationships also influence who we are, what we believe in, how we handle certain situations, how we move, and most importantly, how we take on addictions. Nothing is stronger than the opinion and sway of the ones you love. So, it comes to reason that if there are some gaps and shaky parts in your current or past relationships, they could contribute to nasty habits and obsessions.

From Smartphone to Server

When we are born, we walk, well, crawl into our first relationships; those with our parents, guardians, or caregivers. They are the first to teach and introduce us to things. No matter how the relationship was, we took pieces from them and put them into who we are and how we deal with certain things and feelings. They have a prominent role in influencing us because they were all that we had, along with some other family members and friends of friends. But, you know, in my case, mom and dad were everything...

Because of those reasons above, the ones who took care of you when you were still young and very influential are the first building blocks you have to pull apart.

When you look into a home where the parenting strategies and be-haviors regarding internet use are open, unlimited, unsupervised, and so forth, you will note significant effects. When the child gets older, he is more likely to still have those tendencies, feelings, and routines regarding the internet and its use in handling it. The same goes for a home environment that is not that nice for the child's mental and psychological health, where the trauma and problems make him more prone to addiction.

Before we jump the gun, I am not blaming anyone's parents or guard-ians and telling you that you were brought up wrong. I am also not saying that you are, by any means, raising your child toward an internet addiction. I am simply giving you what the researchers have noted.

Your objections and disagreements are valid. I do not want to upset anyone. These are just things we are looking at and considering to help you out.

In fact, there is nothing wrong with teaching your kids about technology and the internet, but teaching them some guidelines, the dark side, and internet addiction is also an essential part of the deal. Internet addiction disorder, as said before, is a relatively new thing that is still under debate. It is not something as typical as hearing about the dangers of drugs. So, no one is to blame! It is, however, our responsibility to educate the ones we love and do what we will with what we learn here today.

So, onwards and upwards! Your relationships, no matter your beliefs and opinions, affect you and how you handle your addiction from here on out.

This is merely an example, but for argument's sake, let's say there were occasional conflicts in your home. Whenever it popped up, you turned to playing games on the computer or talking to someone on Myspace or Whatever-Chat. It makes sense that this could become a habitual way of dealing with future conflicts, such as a fight you have with your partner. We tend to repeat things if they are a source of comfort or part of our routines.

Patterns: This is all I am talking about. We create them as soon as we are no longer *goo-goo-gawing* around, and we can think and decide for ourselves. Patterns, as their definition implies, repeat until they are busted. These rituals also do not have to come just from your parents alone. You could have stitched them when you were in high school or college or after you had your family. There is no set place to look at, sadly.

Our friends and romantic relationships are the second most influential bonds we come across. We care what our lovers and friends think because we want to feel like we belong in a crowd and are not alone in this world or considered an abnormality. Therefore, even when we are not exposed to the internet at home, its whispers are still around.

Think about when you were in school. If your friends joined an online gaming clan or signed up for a popular social media profile—you were all ears! We wanted to be accepted into our groups and not be the odd ones left out. I do not even remember, but I think we all just wanted to be *cool* or whatever lingoes and motivations we had as children. We were children, after all, and that is what we did.

It is no one's fault, but it leaves a mark on us, whether we like to admit it or not. Sometimes, even when we are adults and probably older, we still want this sense of belonging and being *cool*. So we turn to what we know and what had worked before: The internet. *It was a foolproof plan back in the day, so why not give it a try, for old times' sake?* Many of us feel this way because turning to newer faces and more manageable crowds to please is better, especially when things in the real world are not looking that bright.

It is a mystery why we care so much about what others think, even with all those online quotes telling us to "be ourselves" regardless of what the world says. It has something to do with the thought of being alone and rejected. Which, I am sure you know, are the worst feelings. They are not my favorites, to say the least. Then, we found a way of coping behind a screen, which got us here.

Look, I can try but will fail if I were to give you a direct diagnosis and synopsis of what relationships affected you, how, and when in life. No two people are the same, and I know I say this a lot, but only you can trace and pinpoint the tie-ups that influenced your addiction and ways the most.

When you find those specific or general types of relationships, you will start to see patterns and similarities in your present relationships and how it all contributes to why you use the internet as your way of coping or whatever your reason for the addiction might be. Patterns, once again; it all lies with them.

This essential process will reveal a lot about the person you are and all the peripheral things you carry around. Look, I know what you are thinking. Lots of you are probably cringing uncontrollably and mentally, maybe even physically, losing your lunch at the thought of deep diving and searching around your past and relationships. But you know what they say, you cannot make progress without going through all that icky, uncomfortable, and challenging stuff from time to time. So, do not worry, I got you, and I promise we will get through this together, maybe even with your dinner intact!

Before Google Maps

Another significant reason for internet addiction is where you were brought up, what the people around you were like, how and what they did, and what you were exposed to. In short, your surroundings, environment, and all the backdrops in between pinned their location right onto you.

Your relationships and your environments often go hand in hand. I do not want to blabber on again while on repeat. Therefore, I will try and keep things short.

History and research have shown that your environment significantly affects your life and the risk of addiction and relapse. If you look at any drug-focused film, you will know all you need to know (not literally, though). The point is various places, and things could have influenced your addiction to the internet, even when it was not on purpose.

Once again, everything mentioned previously in the relationship section is also applicable here. You have relationships across a variety of environments. In the home you grew up in, for example, as mentioned before, the people around you influence you profoundly. There were plenty of people like your parents and siblings around you. If you were constantly on the internet or working with tech, you might find some comfortability and familiarity in both of these activities at your home.

Later, you added your teachers, friends, peers, and social group to the mix. On top of that, all the tech and internet lying around on the roads and sidewalks.

Everything works the same, more or less, but I would say that for this section, everything is more general. Do not focus on a direct influence from a single individual. Instead, think of what was around you and what was happening in that space or room.

To give you a better understanding, take your days at school. You might not have known all your peers, but they still had a prominent influence on you. You were intrigued by their interests and what they were up to, and you just wanted to fit in with them. I mean, no one likes sitting empty-handed in a classroom where everyone is on their phones. Maybe, in some cases, your days were not as packed with the internet and tech, but still. It is just an example, so do not lose touch with the point.

As illustrated before, we all wanted to fit in with the fads. We did not want to feel like we were different or missing out on anything. As I have said before, it is just something we do. So, let's say, back then, your environment affected you in such a way, and without you knowing it, it stuck around in the back of your mind. Then you carry it over onto another, more formal and educational setting. Take your days at college or your current work, for example.

It is safe to assume that we are not children anymore. Still, now we have, more than ever, an environment bustling with internet, connectivity, tech, and so on. You could say that almost everyone has online footprints and is latching on to some screen.

So, now we have more general influences flooding into our lives, such as those from our coworkers, family members, peers, and friends. All of them are connected to specific settings in our lives. Everyone, no matter what their age, is obsessed. They use these gadgets and networks for work, entertainment, communication, and almost everything. And still, we find that we want to be a part of it all and not miss out on anything happening around us, just like when we were kids at school. Similarly, we take certain environments and move our habits from one to the next.

I remember this one time, long ago, when I had switched jobs. With the former gig, I had to use my phone a lot. At the new place, however, this was not particularly welcomed. I do not want to go into too much detail, but I can tell you that within those first few weeks, I got into more trouble than I would have liked and could have anticipated. It was a habit I had to break, and it is the perfect example of how we take our practices with us to environments that are similar to those we marked off in our heads. Mine was connecting my cell phone to a work environment. *Oops.*

Another major backer is that our environment is becoming more and more internet and tech-focused in the eye of the media, which has become a giant environment that is around us all the time. The exposure is unprecedented. No matter where you turn, whether turning on the TV or looking over at a billboard, you see ad after ad talking about the latest and best smartphone on the market or that new online game that is taking the world by storm!

Then, when you unlock your phone or go on the internet, you see pop-ups and articles about how this person's Instagram is blowing up because of their magnificent vacation photos or how you can become this and that if you download this app. If you have children, you do not need your phone or any advertisements, as their word-of-mouth is non-stop.

All of this, along with a growing opinion that you genuinely exist only if you are online and that if you do not document your life and events with photos and videos—it never happened. In my opinion, this is an unfair and ridiculous thought, but regardless of what I think, it is a belief that lives.

We have become so used to using the internet and all these devices in our everyday lives that there is no line to break, and some of us just do not know what our environment without them will be like. It all starts with focusing on what you are doing in your surroundings. Some of the best examples are kicking your shoes off at home or burning the midnight oil at work. When you know your rituals and habits, you can stop them from happening and create better ways of doing things, even when the same spaces stick around.

The Problems We Hold

We are more susceptible to addiction when dealing with unresolved feelings, problems, internal struggles, and mental distress or when we stumble when trying to deal with our day-to-day lives, whether at home, work, or any other obligation we have on our plate.

When it comes to psychological aspects and having more gaps in our emotional and mental identities, we have more vulnerabilities dragging us toward the chance of addiction.

When we have pending conflicts getting in our way or other mental health concerns, we might find it harder to ditch our dependency on our addiction. Mental health concerns such as depression, bipolar, anxiety, attention-deficit/hyperactivity disorder (ADHD), or post-traumatic stress disorder (PTSD) are more complicated, mainly because we have more risk tugging at our seams.

Dealing with an internet or technology addiction without any mental health concerns or other behavioral matters is hard enough as it is. When you throw those aspects into the bunch, the intensity and hardships increase to some degree.

You could be fine one minute, and then the very next, you are in this rut you cannot seem to get out of. It is perfectly normal to have your off days and better days, with or without tension brewing on the inside. However, when there is some strain, your bad days might come more often and fiercely than they would for someone without any underlying concerns. Therefore, you need to address these concerns to have a fair shot of taking on your internet and tech addiction the right way without any other problems stepping in your way.

I know you are probably thinking a million different things right now. Perhaps you are skittish about what others think, unsure how to break the news to your loved ones, or you simply feel weak, confused, or embarrassed to admit that you have some problems. However, it is essential to note that there is nothing wrong with having these thoughts, feelings, and tribulations. It happens to the best of us, as they say, and just like an addiction, they are manageable. Sometimes, however, you just need some help to get you on the right road and support you with an added tug or two.

So, why not start by talking to your loved ones; they love you. I mean, it is in that statement alone. They will come around even if they might not understand it at first. Even if things go sideways, at least you got it out, tried, and never know; they might surprise you. After that, gather as much support as possible before you seek professional help, which could assist you in tracking down the next steps you must take to battle your inner demons before you take on your internet fiend.

When There Is More

Furthermore, other factors might come into play as to why we become addicted to our tech and the internet. No matter what has gotten you addicted to these things, it is all within the warning signs. If you were to go back in time, all you had to do was take a closer look at things such as:

- Addictions are often common in some families and often involve genetic inclination. When you have someone in your family closely addicted to the internet and their ways of tech, or even some other forms of addiction, you are at greater risk of taking on the habit yourself.

- Some believe that your gender also plays an essential part in your addiction. It is said that men are more likely to have problems with addictions, while the progression of said addiction is faster in females.

- Suppose you already have a history of going overboard and becoming dependent on things like shopping or drinking caffeine. In that case, you are more likely to become addicted to the internet and your tech. Never say that something is harmless or that you cannot become addicted to it; anything can become addictive if you let it. You are not a "freak" if you have an addictive personality, not at all. It is just something you should look after carefully.

It is as if everything around us has turned into a giant computer. Everything surrounding us keeps screaming that the internet and tech are everything and anything good! It makes lives more comfortable and is amusing, marvelous, something we have within arms-reach. It is the invention of a lifetime, created for its people!

So, we use it without considering for ourselves, "Maybe this is not as good for me as everyone says." You do not stop to think that it is something that can control you. After all, it is not like someone had slapped a warning sticker on the internet. No one anticipated addiction, but as we know, it happens. More often than we think. But, I guess when the world around you throws the keyboard your way, all that is left to do is for you to press ESC.

Chapter 3:

Lasting Lesions

As with any addiction, we know that obsession has lasting side effects. Internet addiction is no different. We are all just living things that need to care for our bodies correctly, or something just does not tick and turn as it should.

Often, when an addiction surrounds our daily lives, we focus our time and effort on the fixation alone, and the rest of our needs and necessities, we slip to the side. We do not always notice them at first. Still, sometimes these effects linger and stick around for the long run.

Sleeping Servers

Internet addiction often leads to fewer hours of shut-eye and poorer sleep quality. Sleep, as all our parents and doctors have groaned, is essential. If you are a sleep *aficionado* like me, you need no reason.

However, if *sleeping when I am dead* is more your style, then I will tell you why you might need to hit the snoozer more often from time to time.

Since we are all about tech, why don't we stick to the theme and look at how laptops work, or at least how my old one ended up? Laptops, as you probably know, are designed to be mobile, so you charge their battery, and then you are good to go for a few hours. Nothing is alarming there.

However, you get those people who leave their laptops plugged, on the bedside table, reciting movies all night long. Sooner or later, you will note that your battery is not doing the job it used to. It will happen.

Devices are made up of components that are working to keep the gadget running as it should, and with all those chores, heat comes and goes. As a result of this constant overheating, the battery's lifespan is often fried. One day you will find that you can barely get in 20 minutes of screen time before having to plug in the chump again and again. Trust me, I know. In my defense, I had fallen asleep while working some nights, and I was a different person back then.

In any case, I am veering off course. We are not here to talk about your battery's life and tech *don'ts*. We are here to talk about our bodies and what sleep does to them.

With that in mind, our bodies are like laptops in that they cannot be overdriven and over-pushed for extended hours without them taking a hit or two. We often take after-hours to pump our bodies with "heat" and "chores" before leaving them to fend for themselves with a few minutes of rest. Then, the next day, it is all about the rewinds and repeats.

We cannot expect our bodies to be at their best behaviors when we do not allow them to shut down, recharge, and cool down. A good night's sleep keeps us mentally and physically healthy and ensures everything is in tip-top shape! So, take the former statement, remove the respite, and you are left with a "battery" with a damaged lifespan.

Still, why am I blaming the internet and tech for lack of sleep? Well, because it has become such a norm in our lives. So much that we tend to forget to put them on the side and switch them off ourselves. In return, we invest more time on the internet by the day and ditch our sleep. On top of that, they directly clash with how we sleep, causing those long nights of tossing and turning.

Think about it when you go to bed. Do you have a TV in your room playing away to soothe you into your slumber? Are you bustling away on your phone before you turn it in? What is your pre-bed routine like, and does it include some sort of tech or online setup?

If you use any device with a screen, you are exposing yourself to blue light. When this light shoots into your eyes, your body produces less of the so-called sleep hormone, melatonin, which tells you when it is time to hit the hay. After only an hour and a half of exposure, you block this hormone from releasing into your body. So, you might as well kiss the roof hello, as you will be staring at it all night long.

Another thing about using the internet and tech before bed is that they are activities that "run away" when we use them. You might have started playing a game or scanning through Facebook early, but it was all about just one more stage, or another post will not hurt! Before you can even fluff your pillow, the clock strikes midnight.

We are not supposed to use the internet and tech for at least 30 minutes before planning to go to bed. It can be hard when you are addicted to them or already have a sleeping disorder. You might feel some discomfort and restlessness not having these activities. Yet, I can promise they are doing more harm than good, and counting sheep is much better than counting SSDs!

Online and Alone

We know there is a glamor in the internet that sweeps you off your feet and away from all the problems and responsibilities life inevitably brings your way. I know it feels great at first, talking to people online and losing yourself in a world of games and entertainment. However, this high does not last and eventually leaves you alone in front of a dim screen, scrolling through simulated profiles you envy.

Self-isolation is this self-withdrawal from the real world, its people, and everything outside of the personal bubble you have created for yourself. It is a self-destructive way of cutting yourself off from what is around you, what you are missing out on, and the chances of creating meaningful relationships and memories.

This solitary choice of living also has a lot of other effects on your life, as you are no longer focusing on what the world has to show. You are wasting it in front of TVs and smartphones instead of embarking on adventures and activities as you should. Which really is not living, just floating in the cloud.

It might not always be just that the internet is better, though. Some of us find creating connections with others in real life tough and sometimes chewy—we are socially awkward, shy, or never quite know the right words to say. Where do you even go to make friends these days? Struggles like these already block you into a life of seclusion, while the internet is the final punch that only worsens the blow.

We find comfort and joy in pretending we do not want anything other than those relationships we have typed out. Yet, I believe that all of us crave these physical, face-to-face bonds and experiences with others. We are a species designed to love, care, and share ourselves with others and accept them into our own circles. When we do not allow ourselves to feel nourished with these ties and relations, we are slowly fragmenting our mental health and stability.

I do not care about the number of followers you have, how many people DM you daily, or whether, at this moment, you feel okay with your choice of sticking to virtual friends. Someday you will feel this burning ick of wanting to go grab a cup of coffee with a friend, and when you turn to call someone, you realize no one is around. I do not want this for you, and I know that you do not want it for yourself, deep down, behind the profiles and chat apps.

Depression Database

We all have those off days where we just feel blue and want nothing more than to stay in bed and brood. I have those days, too, so you do not have to feel as though you are alone. It is when this gloom grows and spreads into more days that are the same; however, you have to consider whether it is a hurdle in your life or perhaps something that cuts deeper. Something like depression.

Depression is a serious condition that affects millions of people around the world. There is no solid explanation for why it is around at all. Sometimes, it is genetic, and other times, it results from various biological and environmental factors that run through our lives.

It is also a part of internet addiction because of various reasons and events leading up to it, such as when you self-isolate. As an article by Caroline Miller stated, "Experts see the rise in depression as evidence that the connections social media users form electronically are less emotionally satisfying" (2022). I know this statement does not cover the wide world of the internet, but it gives us an idea of how online lives will never measure up to living presently in your own environment.

Depression sometimes already exists in the back of someone's mind, and we think that the internet has made us depressed. While other times, something like your overuse of the internet and the loss of real-life connections and links causes depression. Either way, the fact stands that you need to call out for help and do what it takes to show depression who's the boss and that you are taking back control of your happiness.

But, as you know, we have to learn more about the situation before we can take the steps, so here they are:

The internet gives us a world of knowledge, entertainment, and possibilities, all within a click. It is extraordinary to have such access to unlimited cultures, movements, and information. However, sometimes things get overwhelming, and our minds cannot process and handle the herds of information trekking our way. This event is commonly known as "information overload." Because our brains are *cool* that way, they adapt.

However, this is not always a good transformation. Our brains start running in overdrive as it thinks this is how it has to stay to keep up with the rate of things. Life, which is already a pretty busy thing, picks up speed, and now, when we take a break, things feel... boring.

So, we turn to our gimmicks to remove these feelings of lethargy. We go back to a place where we are much more susceptible to depression.

No single cause or internet activity is sparking this reaction in your brain. It could be that you feel jealous of the people on social media: How good their lives look, how happy and lucky they are, and how you wish your life could be like that. This sends you down a rabbit hole of judgment, critique, and loathing. You get depressed because things in your life are just not looking up. You think, "*What am I doing wrong? Am I not as special? Why them and not me?*"

Perhaps, you just enjoy social media and the social drops you have created. When you are away from them, you just feel down and anxious, awaiting your next login. The same goes for other interactions such as online gaming, virtual chat rooms, etc. You need them to lift you up and be that presence in your life that is, in truth, lacking.

Maybe, you have just found this escapism that works to keep the depression and realities at bay. Porn, gaming, blogging, reading, and playing with the search engine, these are just some examples. Whatever it may be, you thrive on those dopamine boosts they give you, and you hate how it gets flushed afterward. You want to feel "normal" and be in your best mood every day because, quite frankly, no one wants to feel as though their energy has been slurped away from them, as if there is a dark cloud thundering above their heads, and that there is a numbed sadness left behind.

These dopamine rises are the only reason these activities are around and why you feel the way you do. They are, however, a short-term fix, not a treatment. You can still take life by the horns, though. Depression is tolerable and treatable when needed, and it is not something that has to last in some people. You are the writer of your story. Maybe for now, just stick to writing on paper!

Chapter 4:

The Manual of Symptoms and Signs

B y now, we know each other rather generously. Well, at least you know I tend to ramble on and overtalk. Therefore, I have decided to switch things up with a straight-to-the-point manual of symptoms and signs you should look out for because you might be a tech junkie who needs help to get clean. With that said, you mustn't stop because your answer came back unsatisfactory. You need help now more than ever. Allow yourself that.

However, I must caution you against self-diagnosing some of these symptoms. Please do not Google them. I know I cannot stop you, so if you do, you will be diagnosed with something else. For starters, it would be best to go check it out, even if the diagnosis might be far-stretched; peace of mind is a heck of a pill. Also, you never know; the symptom checks might have been suitable for once, but don't always believe what you read on the internet!

Furthermore, just to give you a quick user manual on using these signs and symptoms to self-diagnose, simply mark out all of those applicable to you and your situation. Put your life under a microscope and really think about whether or not you have some signs and symptoms of internet addiction. Remember to be genuine and honest with yourself, or else what is the point? This is not a test or public confession. It is a safe place for you and you alone (unless you want to share). Today, we are simply putting you, your health, and your future first.

Emotional Indications

Let's start by identifying our emotional indicators.

- Depression and feelings of sadness (especially when you are not using tech, online, or connected).

- You are dishonest when confronted by others and asked about your internet and tech usage.

- You feel guilty and somewhat repentant about your internet and tech use and neglect of others and responsibilities.

- Anxiety and agitation (especially when without internet and tech).

- Feelings of bliss when using gadgets and the internet, as if you are on some kind of elevated high.

- You often feel alone and you tend to isolate yourself.

- You have mood swings and emotional withdrawal symptoms when you are without the internet and your gizmos.

- You become somewhat bored with your everyday life (you find tasks and routines tedious and you are not interested in certain events anymore).

- You feel scared and alarmed when you think about yourself in the real world or without your phone and a way of being connected.

- You often feel as though you are drained of your energy and never quite rested even after you have been to bed.

- You often feel "lost" in your life especially when you are not distracted by the web and tech.

Physical Manifestations

Besides the emotional stabs an internet addiction takes on you, you will also feel how the effects play with your body. Most of these symptoms are caused by how you use the internet and how much time you spend on your devices; however, others are plain because they become your world.

- Back and neck pain (from a poor hunched posture in front of a screen and lack of moving around).

- Carpal tunnel syndrome (pinched nerve in the wrist causes numbness, tingling, and pain in the hand and arm).

- Headaches (sometimes accompanied by fever).

- Insomnia and other sleep disorders or problems sleeping.

- Skimpy eating patterns (poor nutrition, missing meals, overeating), that often lead to weight loss, putting on some pounds, or getting ill more frequently.

- Lack of personal care (not washing up regularly or staying in the same outfit for days on end, not grooming yourself, losing interest in your appearance, and experiencing problems with self-image).

- Problems with vision and dry, sore eyes from staring at the screen.

Time Manifestations

Time management, on a good day, is a hard thing to stick to. Sometimes, we find ourselves doing something, and the next thing we have planned just disappears. It happens to the best of us every now and again. However, when an addiction creeps into your life, you tend to fall short of personal matters, responsibilities, and obligations, all because you value your time on the internet more. Even at times when you do not plan to take the clock that far.

- You cannot keep schedules (cannot control time spent on the internet and devices and cannot move around using them for real-life obligations and plans).

- You struggle to prioritize that which is necessary; instead, you rank your internet use as the most essential part of your life.

- You have no sense of time (especially when using the internet), and you often do not stick with plans or are often late to appointments.

- Procrastination (of responsibilities, tasks, commitments, and sleep).

- You have more and more skipped days from work or classes.

- Others, such as your boss or partner, have voiced concerns about your tardiness and lack of "presence" while off the internet.

- Your devices and internet use takes up most of your time, and you find yourself unable to stop and manage your time.

Before I sign off and we move over to the next chapter, I wanted to take the time to get some things off my mind. First and foremost, it is essential to note that symptoms and signs of internet addiction are not limited to those listed above. Some people may experience other feelings and manifestations, such as dosing themselves with different energy lifters, such as energy drinks, caffeine, pills, and the whole lot, which holds loads of other health effects. Therefore, you should not limit yourself and your self-diagnosis to what I have given you.

The most essential part of self-diagnosing is listening to yourself and what your gut is telling you. If you feel that the internet and your electronic devices are moving your life or that you have a problem (even when you have none of these symptoms), stick to your hunch. You know yourself best, after all, so you would notice if something just does not fit right.

I also wanted to take the time to acknowledge the help from some people and entities who helped me lay out the manual. Full credit goes to them where needed, of course. So, with that said, I would like to thank Christina Gregory, Oasis Recovery Runcorn, Manor Clinic, and Primrose Lodge.

Chapter 5:

Little Known Reasons, Revealed

◆━━━━━━━●━━━━━━━◆

We now know what you are up against, what keeps you plugged in, and what might have caused you to turn on that computer in the first place. However, one more piece of the image must be colored in: *What drove you to do this?*

I can repeat as many factors and how addiction works as I like, but the true answer to the question starts and lies only with you. You know who you are. You know the things you are dealing with. The circumstances you are in and what drives your addiction from the core and out all start and end with you. No matter how cheesy that might sound.

Breaking an addiction is not about proving to others what you can do and what you are capable of; specifically, you are one of those people who can show the addiction *who's the boss*. Yes, you are capable of anything, and you can most definitely kick the addiction to the curb! However, you will have to do this: Break the addiction for yourself and with yourself in mind, or else you will just take it out on the ones you love, and you will never indeed be ready to give up that part of you, no matter how many times you try and convince yourself otherwise.

Your reason can be that you feel you never spend time with your loved ones, but it should still be a conscious choice and decision, even when your motive is to treat others the right way. I cannot tell you why you have to take on this journey or what you should do, although I can definitely try, and help you where I can, of course. You will have to sit by yourself and figure out the reasons behind your change of heart and why you have decided to throw the power supply down the drain!

Trust that you know best simply because you do. Believe in yourself because you are capable of so much more than drowning yourself in posts and notifications and setting up bios and Instagram feeds. You deserve to have a fighting chance to change your fate and future so that in the end, when the clouds come to scrape you up along with them, you can look back at your life and know that you lived every second to its fullest and the way you wanted without regrets and a screen standing in place of your headstone. I know, melancholy, perhaps, but true. Life will pass you by if you do not take your eyes off the keys, and I can promise you that it will never be worth it.

Therefore, you must take a magnifying glass to what you have read in all the chapters above and use them to your advantage. Learn more about your addiction and how the internet clouds our lives. Learn more about yourself, why you are here, and how you got tangled up in the wires of modern technologies. Lay out your foundations and gain the self-awareness you need to become the person you are meant to be.

It is crucial to ensure that you have a plan that will work and everything in place before you dive into how you can take on these strategies, actions, and tasks that will guide you through your detox and new life. Without knowing the basics of all you are and your internet addiction, it might become harder for you to truly step into the second step of your journey, which is self-management. If not, you might find that the hurdles are too significant to jump over and that playing it smart might not be enough.

Take a chance on yourself and leave the tech and internet behind simply because you do not need it; in fact, you never did. You just needed something or someone to give you that nudge to snap you back to where you belong. If you have not felt that pinch yet, this is it. This is your wake-up call, or whatever you want to call it. So, before you start the run, learn to crawl by looking into your life and who you are. It is essential; I promise you that. You will only be able to disconnect, unplug, avoid distractions, and finally regain control over your life. So, what are you waiting for? You have your guide, your sign, and everything else you could need to succeed. So, go out and take your life back from the hands of the net!

STEP TWO:

SELF-MANAGEMENT JUMPING HURDLES AND PLAYING IT SMART

Chapter 6:

Disaster Recovery

◆•————————•————————•◆

I know the past few chapters of the book so far have not been on the *happy-go-lucky* side of things. However, I am pleased to tell you that the heavy-hearted talks are finally over! You have just turned onto a new page and a new section where your internet addiction and all that goes with it can be slapped onto your rearview mirror. Up next is your digital detox!

What Is It Anyway?

Detoxification is "a regimen or treatment intended to remove toxins and impurities from the body" (Merriam-Webster, 1847b). A digital cleanse works the same way, more or less, as you are ridding yourself and your life of the dangers and side effects of internet addiction and overuse.

It is time to step into the real world and enjoy all it offers, away from all the screens and buttons. In the end, that is all a digital detox is:

Intentionally taking some time to reduce your internet and tech usage while allowing yourself to repair some areas in your life, snap back to reality, and look after yourself, your health, and others.

A disaster recovery roadmap begins with removing the cables and plugs attached to you and breaking free from the USBs. This is the final step you have to take.

Before You Pull the Plug

The process of detoxing yourself from the digital world is much like shutting down your computer. It is not always as simple and swift as it looks. Beneath the swirling circle, a lot is going on.

Upon clicking the 'off' button, the computer runs through a series of steps and processes to ensure that your work, programs, and systems are safe and secure. After that, your operating system is downed before the power goes out.

Much like a computer, your body cannot shut down from the digital world without first running through some processes of its own. You have some checking to do in certain areas, programs and processes to close, and places to log out, which, in reality, just means you have some more understanding to gain of how and why a digital detox works. You have some steps to take before you can move forward in your life and determine how you can get where you want to go.

You will definitely experience some withdrawal symptoms, challenges, and barriers along your road, but in the end, you will walk out the other side with a sunburn instead of a smartphone. So many opportunities await you; the key to unlocking it all is stepping away from the internet, tech, and the hold it has on you.

However, considering you have already made it this far, I think it is safe to say you already knew that and that you are already locked and ready for change. So, why don't we get down to it and clean you up?!

How It Helps?

We have learned quite a lot about what makes us tick and why internet addiction and tech overuse can make it all slow down. In short, I could have summed it down to a single point: It is no good for you and others!

Internet addiction and tech use takes a great deal out of your life and demand a lot from you. By now, you might have realized to what extent your life has been impacted by the blue lights and keys you push, and hopefully, you are genuinely on the hunt for change.

If you are still not convinced, let me put it this way: When you turn the tables and choose to remove this destructive force from your life, everything else, too, will fall into place. Balance and stability will be restored as positive change pours toward you. Your life will be the way it should have been before the tech. The best part of the deal is that you are at the front of the wheel!

Real Time Reconnecting

We know that an internet addiction takes a toll on your social life, relationships, and presence in the real world and even moves those around you. One moment you are browsing online stores, and the next, you lose yourself and your loved ones in the sight of the keyboard. Okay, perhaps it will not happen that fast, but still.

When you remove the internet and its supporting tech, you will find that all those pieces you lost or tore will slowly be sewn back together.

You get the chance to enjoy time with yourself and those around you. You get to create and submerge yourself in fulfilling relationships while shaping up and rebuilding those you have lost or hurt by your addiction. It offers you your second chance to step in and focus on what you value in your life and show the people you love how much you care.

It also means taking the time to take care of and love yourself. Who you are on the internet does not have to be all you are. While also taking care of your ties, you must remember who you are and why you deserve to be happy. It is an essential part of the process. Without loving yourself, you will never truly grasp loving others the right way, or at least, that is what I think. Over and above that, you deserve to love yourself without guilt and feeling *weird* about it.

When they say that relationships are meant to go both ways, they often mean that both parties of a couple have to give their all. However, here it also means that you should focus not only on your relationships with others but your relationship with yourself. Look after both bonds, and they will look after you.

Furthermore, you will no longer feel alone, blocked out from the world, and as if you are "missing out" on everything everyone else is experiencing because you no longer are. You are finally free from the smartphone cases holding you back. You are stepping out there and showing the world what you've got. There is so much more to life than video games and Instagram posts, but I guess you will come to find them on your own.

The Therapy Chair

An internet addiction also strains your life and health. As you know, many symptoms and effects come with the obsessive need to stay online and stay charged. When you remove the stressor, you will pull some weight off your shoulders. And the other arrears of your life that have been impacted by your dependence are your professional career, education, and marital and familial affair.

It is all about clutching back control over your life and remapping everything to fit your needs and desires. You can, for example, finally catch up on some much-needed sleep, which will also help you take on the day with more energy and up your mental and physical health. Perhaps you can jot up a bucket list of things you have always wanted to do before grabbing life by the horns and finally getting in the time you have missed while stuck in front of the computer. You will finally be able to get to all your responsibilities and obligations while sticking to meetings, appointments, and all the things you have dropped, delayed, and procrastinated. I cannot promise that everything will be perfect. However, it is worth a shot, and I can promise you it will be better than this. It is an improvement that everyone else will also see unfolding. It is a shot worth taking.

You have the opportunity to remove yourself from the penitentiary that holds you glued in. The accurate way of getting back your life and pulling more and more from what the world has to offer you is by ultimately taking steps to ensure that you live without the distractions of the online world.

Prep for Conquest

Before we can jump into a detox, some prep work is still left to do. Think of a steak, you can tuck and soak the meat in layers of spices and marinade, but when it comes to the actual cooking, you have to consider more: The heat of the stove, the oil you use, and the level of doneness you have to push for, especially when you are cooking for more than one because not everyone likes their plate oozing with blood.

Leaping into detox is like cooking a steak until it is well-done, medium, or rare. Not everyone likes it the same way, and not everyone can toss their tech into the bin whenever they feel like it. A lot of us still need some answers and a plan of action as some kind of insurance.

Therefore, the first step of prep would be to ask yourself questions, do some evaluations, and work through all the grub before you get to all the good stuff.

Why don't we start with the former and get down to some questions you have to answer as a foundation for your cleanse:

Realistic Reports

Think about what you are getting out of your device. What does it take from you, and why do you want to dump the net? Are there things you want more time for, people you want to catch up with? What are some of the benefits you will get once the devices are gone? What is your reason for wanting to take this step toward a cleaner tomorrow? Genuinely think about how you use your phone, the habits surrounding them, and your answers before writing them down, or simply think about them in your head and then answer them to the best of your abilities. Although, I would advise you to keep a record of them so that, later down the road, you can look back at them for motivational means.

You also have to take in your life and daily routine. A detox for someone who works with books the whole day would look a lot different than someone who needs to be on their computer 24-7. Sometimes things just are not realistic, and they do not fit into what our lives look like. If the 24-7 people were to go off-grid for a week, chances are, yes, they will get a good detox, but they will also need to do some job searching right after. Keep things feasible and practical, and make the detox work for you.

I am not saying to blow off your detox just because you have some work; you can still pump the gas on more minor, simple changes while concentrating, working out your priorities, and sending an advance notice your boss's way.

The first part of preparing for your detox is throwing together a sort of report on yourself and your life, including how it would look if you were without the tech and internet, or at least, at this stage, how you hope it would look. You have to choose the right sort of detox and the correct time frame, and then set up an executive summary of all the plans and actions you are going to take before giving everyone a shout about what you are all about and finally disembarking on your detox.

You have to decide what you want to do and how you want to do it. However, a bit of guidance never hurt anyone. Well, apart from the children in the *Pied Piper* tale. But that is a whole other book.

No Distractions

When you are distracted, you are more likely to give in to your tech and internet temptations or ultimately fail altogether. So, with that said, as soon as you remove the distractions from the equation, you will have a better shot at getting things right.

When it comes to removing distractions caused by technology, you need to remove the actual devices from your surroundings and yourself. You could, for example, turn off your notifications while taking some time for yourself while setting up specific times when you can go to catch up on them. You could always go out with some friends for lunch when you feel tempted, or perhaps you can take on some cooking, journalling, or other activity that acts as a rewarding replacement. You could even try putting some space between you and your device, such as leaving it in the other room while you are working out, or in designated "no-tech" areas, such as the dinner table or bed.

Independency from Technologies

With the addiction and overuse of the internet, we shape a dependency on our devices, up to the point where they are not only a part of our lives, but we cannot get through the day without them. You cannot undergo a digital detox if you cannot remove yourself from the tech. Although I will not lie, it might be hard at first, but eventually, you will get to where you have to go.

Remember how I mentioned making more minor, manageable changes at the start? Well, that is, especially now, what I am talking about. While prepping, you are not cooking the entire steak from the get-go; you chop your onions and cut up the garlic cloves. Recipes are separated for a reason, and it is no different when it comes to other things in life. You have to focus on preparing yourself for your time without the internet, not dive into the deep end without your lifebuoy.

Removing the internet's hold on you starts with sorting out your life and the tech surrounding you. Remember, we are still technically compiling a report and summary of your life, so you have to be able to notice your smartphone usage, your screen time, and the so-called 'problem areas' you are finding particularly hard to let go of.

For argument's sake, let's say you depend on your phone to wake you up and entertain you in the bathroom or while you are on your lunch break. I say depend because you cannot seem to do these things without your tech in hand; they feel off and more rushed. Therefore, for you to successfully become disconnected, you need to unpack your technology's functionality and replace it with more gadget-free alternatives.

Go retro and grab a physical alarm clock to ring you up in the mornings, a newspaper or book to read for the bathroom, pickle a crossword puzzle, or haul a friend for your lunch break. It is crucial to have these bursts of tech-free times and intervals when you cannot do otherwise, such as when you need a laptop for work or call clients the whole day. Just because you have a day demanding the internet and devices does not mean you cannot tiptoe towards more extended periods without them.

Even when you do not have to use tech for work or keep in touch with family who cannot make the drive to your home, you could still be tempted by the flush of emotions and activities your usage brings you. Therefore, your best shot would be to remove them from your life and declutter your devices as much as possible.

For example, you could reduce access to some apps by disabling your accounts or deleting specific programs altogether. Scroll through your camera roll and contacts to see which ones you can drop in the bin.

You could try to track how long you use your tempted apps, such as when you are on social media. You can simply jot down the time before you jump online and note when you climbed off. Some apps help you restrict your time on the phone, but I thought it would be best to keep them out of the solution. Self-control and discipline is the best route to follow.

When things are "cleaner" around you, in your life, and across all your devices, you will find that there are fewer and fewer things tempting you over time. Which is, of course, what we want. I know it might be hard not to hoard those hundreds of hilarious memes you have saved, but they serve you no purpose, so it is time to let them go.

Focus on the Structural Support

Some of us perform better when we have someone on our side cheering us on and letting us know that we can turn to them if needed. Thus, communication is a necessary step in planning your detox.

There are two ways this could be done: Informing those around you of your plans to go off-the-grid for some time, giving them alternative ways of reaching you, as discussed not so long ago, and making plans to meet them in person. While the other way is for people, whether it be your friends, family members, or roommates, to participate in the detox themselves. I am not talking about forcing people to go clean by pulling out the Wi-Fi and shutting off the power to the house. Some people close to you might also be struggling with balancing their lives, and they could find it refreshing to give it all a break and snap away from their everyday life. Talk it out—that is all there is left to do. Even when no one around you is up for the challenge just yet, make sure to find ways you can keep yourself busy while they are distracted by their tech. Inform them of your reasons, motivations, and how you plan to go about your detox so that they can better support you with what they have and know.

Then we have another stick in the structural support that needs addressing: You. We do not need a crowd of spectators and cheerleaders hyping us up and deciding whether or not we will have a good day today. You are perfectly capable of being that person for yourself. All you need is to believe and trust that you've got this under control.

Remind yourself why you are taking the time to unplug, list things you want to do during your detox, write them down, and keep them near. Head out and work in your garden, organize your closet, or catch up with some old friends from college. Remember that you are not losing tech and the internet; you are gaining much more benefits and time to live. Savor every moment, live in the present, and reconnect with what is most important in your life.

Don't be too hard on yourself, either. Devices are little sirens meant to hook their users. Sure, no one wanted or anticipated people to get addicted. Yet, we go back to the devices time and time again. You are not alone in this: Not in your addiction or detox. You are also not meant to be working against yourself, so stop being such a harsh critique.

Keep that in mind whenever you have a slip or off day. Nothing can be perfect, and detox is something that falls right into that category.

As much as I hate to admit it, detoxing is not an easy gig to launch. I cannot tell you how many times I tried the *Lemon Juice Cleanse* before I finally got the hang of it. Detox is not the easiest thing to pull out from under the rug, but it is doable. Being scared and anxious about change and uncertain outcomes is normal and expected, so all you have to do is be courageous.

Where to Divert Your Gaze

As we know, there are different areas of the internet that we grow attached to. Various activities and spoils got us addicted in the first place. While there are three main tech categories we use the most and need some dusting off and wiping clean: Your email, social media, and compulsive internet use. Well, I guess there is not much more to say than that. No matter what your poison is: Gmail, Outlook, Twitter, Instagram, research, or interactive games—all of it will be thrown into a bin and sent off to the laundromat in no time!

Chapter 7:

Managing Mailboxes

◆•————●————•◆

Emails are much more than simple icons of envelopes you find on your screen. They are inventions of communication that have come far since their creation in 1965. They aimed to be a single space where messages and files were brought together and shared, all within a single click. It was email, and it broke barriers all over.

Today, however, the fallback approach has shifted into something more regular and strappy. A bed of roses that some of us occasionally use more than our mouths these days.

Look, I get it, I use email too, and the convenience and simplicity thereof are spectacular! However, the world as we know it has grown into an almost digital brace. With this rise in tech has come an increase in personal and work-related emails, not to mention the junk mail, newsletters, promotions, and spam that get through.

I know loads of people who have no problem running through their emails while leaving thousands unread. I, on the other hand, am not such a person. I find these overcrowded stacks of emails quite over-whelming. They do nothing to help me get through the day and stay on top of my work. After all, I am a busy man—I have emails to re-ceive, some to read, and people to reply to. Many of us do not have the time to scan through dispensable whatnots claiming to be *important*, while they are, in truth, only cluttering up your inbox at the end of the day. Personally, I much instead prefer keeping my space tidy, stacked, and filed.

Sometimes, this is what we all want: A clean, almost new inbox—a mint start without the countless subscription emails, promotional clunk, and emails from who-knows-when. Regardless of what we want, life does not always work that way. One day you skip those four unread lines, and the next moment there are innumerable more added to the collection. It is understandable how your inbox can become a bit too much.

Email overload is "the inability to keep on top of emails" without feeling crowded and swamped (Lau, n.d.). Yet, not all of us know the toll emails take on us and how our lives are affected. So, why don't I enlighten you?

Although tech and software exist to help us break through the sweat of work and chores, they could also easily be grave thieves of our time and productivity. You would not think that something as simple as clicking on a line, reading, and shooting a quick reply would take as much time as it could from you. That is the thing; you barely notice how significantly your inbox can grow and how much time you spend run-ning through all your emails, whether it be addressing them or deleting them. Before you know it, however, within the blink of an eye, your day is over. Not a very productive way of spending your hours, is it?

Every message coming in, going out, or sorted is time you could have spent doing something else and being more productive, whether it be at home or at work.

Let's take the work scenario for a second. Your boss urgently wants a report or client contract sent to you via email. The problem is this: The client has been around for years. You have also talked to his wife and assistant from time to time. That makes it three recipients to track down and years of communication to run through. You have tried everything! You've used different subject lines, keywords, and contacts and searched through individual emails without anything relevant popping up. The file is nowhere. It means you have lost days of work searching for something that is gone—a pointless search.

There is also the fact that you have misplaced information because of your cramped online workspace. It happens often, the loss of conversations, attachments, and tasks amid a chaotic inbox, scrambled with vital files and mails that you would much rather keep in the trash.

An overfilled inbox could also cause problems in how people trust you with communication and reliability. People, including you and I, do not like being ignored; we despise it. Think about when you reach out to a business only to receive a reply weeks later or none at all. You feel this irritating push on your emotions, and you would never reach out to them again, or am I wrong?

Well, you have to take what you can give out, and if your communication is a bit on the slow side, you could quickly become that "week later reply guy" that would not get a message or second thought. It could impact your professional reputation, performance, and ability to grow in your occupation. It can also take a hit on your personal life. Imagine sending your friends and family countless invitations to parties and events or constantly trying to reach out to them without prevailing. Sooner or later, you might feel offended and "touched" by their absence, failure of acknowledgment, and scarcity from your life. They are just like you and will grow tired of your lack of replies. Sure, most friends and family members would give you a call if you are not reacting to their emails, but still.

The only thing you truly need to know about email overload and getting lost in your inbox is that it is not suitable for you. Why would you willingly throw yourself under the stress of a heavy workload, which, in turn, takes a toll on your psyche, emotions, health, and commitments? You would not, or at least I hope not, because you do not deserve to crumble under the poundage of the virtual mailboxes we hold. Sort your things and keep them tidy; life is already stressful enough, and you do not need emails adding to that!

How Did We Get Here

It would seem that email overload happens to the best of us. We live very active lives that are often humming with work and personal matters, so it is understandable how your inbox might get away from you from time to time. Your busy life is, however, not the only factor that comes into play when looking at your overloaded mailbox. Other pins might have pushed your surplus, and today we will look at them all without going into too many details on how to fix your mistakes and keep the envelopes sealed.

Weighing Down the Workspace

We all have responsibilities, dreams, and ambitions, which is why we pursue specific jobs and positions. Well, that and the fact that we do not want to die from starvation. Whatever your motive might be, we all need work and money.

Working is not an easy part of life, and with it comes certain obligations and duties, one of which might involve communicating with clients and coworkers. It is here, within the workplace, that many emails and junk are loaded into our inboxes and stacked onto us. Even when we try our best to stay on top of our incoming and outgoing mail, we get lost in creating invoices, making sales calls, or doing anything else we have to do.

Before we know it, we skimp off our other work because our inboxes are too full. This is the problem with emails: Very few people view them as a form of labor or task we have. It is often disregarded as "something" we occasionally do, do not have to keep an eye on, and goes without any tabs because it is simply not as important as the rest of the work we have on our plates. That is, until your boss asks for an email, file, or whatever. Then you have to spend days scrolling and searching through hundreds of unread emails and forgotten conversations, or you get a call from "the man" asking you why you had not responded to that one client that emailed, whom you accidentally skipped past.

Emailing is work, taking up just as much time and importance, if not more, than any other assignment. It is time you realize that and start treating your inbox, business or personal, the way you should have from the start.

Most of us use time management, organization, lists, and schedules to ensure that our work is done right and on time. Since we have now established that our inability to see emails as actual duties is a weighing factor, we can catch on to how other parts of the job might also need to change.

Your schedule, for example, especially when not considering your email priorities, will have to change in such a way that you set aside some time to look and work through them. This is beneficial for your job performance and reputation as an employee and your personal life, especially if you tend to leave the mail for those nights at the dinner table or Jimmy's soccer practice. For the most part, we tend to stick to schedules; therefore, when emails are not considered a part of the plan, it is easy to see how you could forget about it, which could lead to an email overload.

Then there is you: The factor that could have the most significant effect. We often get in the way of ourselves, especially when it comes to our sense of wanting to be accepted and often praised. Let's face it, no one wants mud smeared on their reputation, and they want to look good in front of their bosses. You try to sprint through your emails to get down to the other work that has you tied up. In the meantime, you are losing productivity that could have been spent doing those other things. That is why sorting your emails and keeping them that way is essential. Otherwise, you will spend hours trying to catch up on hundreds of items that have been gathering dust.

With that said, you should not be afraid of speaking your mind and giving your opinion if you feel that there are some business protocols you disagree with. A business impacts how we handle our emails to a great extent. If your firm's processes are vague, the computers will be flooded with emails, meeting requests, follow-ups, and a bunch of questions. Why not throw your boss a request for a meeting about the protocols and talk it out? It will benefit not only you but the whole company, after all.

Last but not least, the last bit of factors a business holds onto us lies within our specific situations and commitments. Someone who works in a warehouse would have fewer email obligations than someone working as an event planner, for example.

When your job often includes working alongside others or counting on their next moves, you will find you have more emails because of your dependency on the work they offer and give. When it takes two to tango, there has to be more communication and back-and-forth.

If you were to work alone, however, you would find that you have more freedom over what you do when you do it, and to some extent, the level of satisfaction and stress you have to deal with. Nonetheless, these days everything we do has some connection to communication, especially the digital kind. Emails, amongst other things, have become an integral part of our lives.

Still, even when you work independently as a freelancer, business owner, or from home in any capacity, where your personal and business emails commingle, you will find that things are just about the same. That is business as usual for you, I suppose.

When in Home

We know that there is much more to life than just work. Your personal space is meant to be your own, and the overlap of loads of emails is no good. Even when we know we must stay away, sometimes, we cannot help ourselves.

No one wants to miss out or feel as though they are missing out on anything; therefore, you get over-involved in every email that comes your way, just in case something happens.

Most importantly, you know which emails are worth looking at by their subject lines, past the promotional ads and newsletters from your subscribed websites and channels. You would be surprised to find how fast they add up.

Later on, they overflow, and you can no longer keep track of whether or not important emails have come through. When you click a website, you are more often than not forced to subscribe to continue reading an email or use some sort of tool and function on the website itself. We do not always want to go out and search around for a similar, free program/function/article, or you cannot find anything relevant but that one site, so your login/subscription adds another email list to your inbox. This can be pretty overwhelming.

In all, not filtering your messages also caused this overcrowding. Sorting your emails into groups, folders, and categories can lower the chances of disarray. Your email program does not always know which message should go where, which is how essential conversations end up in your spam folder or promotional sends. However, even between the mess, we often skip past the 50% off deals and reminders of new articles, shooting to what we view as essential. Yet, we still miss some messages here and there from time to time.

The same goes for those messages we rely on as little to-do lists. Sure, for the most part, they seem to work. Sometimes, however, we finish a bit of work, leave the rest for later, and before we know it, we lose track of other tasks as the emails flood in. No matter what the lists were about, you will find that they are not only ineffective but are easily lost between the rows of it all.

Sometimes, in pure simplicity, you cannot escape the world of emails and the occasional overload and pressures it brings, no matter what your causes may be. Sometimes, email overload just happens to the best of us.

Mail Sorters

Sorting your emails and taking some time away from the "compose" button is a three-step process where you declutter your inbox, take some time to yourself, and stop the overload from ever happening again. Do not worry; it will not be anything complex or time-consuming. It is instead to the point and simple to get into your life (even when it might not seem like it at the start).

Throwing It Into the Bin

You cannot take your well-deserved break or stop and move on from your email overload without first taking care of the rubbish that has already made its way into your inbox. Therefore, that is precisely what you have to do: Take out the trash and start anew.

As they say, the most obvious place is the best place to start. Okay, perhaps no one, except for me just now, has said that. Nonetheless, that is not the point. You have to start in your inbox. I know the whole point why you are here for this read, and why we are doing this at all, is because we want to steer away from all the emails, folders, and replies, but still. Decluttering is the only way to push yourself in the right direction without a possible overload peeking behind a digital envelope. So, how can you go about doing that?

You will have to run through your entire list of emails, subject line per subject line, before deciding which of them you want to keep and which ones will have to go. I will not deck out and adorn the fact that this part of the process is anything but fun! I personally hated doing this every step of the way. It feels annoying to run through thousands of messages because that is what it is—aggravating. Although, when it is all said, done, and deleted, you will feel "cleaner" since fewer tech-chat are crowding your space and pulling you down. It is about taking control of your life and what goes in and out of your inbox. Seizing the moment, breaking your ties, and all that globe starts with the stuff that chafes us.

Think of this as sorting through an actual file cabinet. Files pile up by the decade's worth, and the best way to sort through them would be to throw them into three categories or stacks. The files you still have to get to, those you can throw to the side, and the ones for the bins. I could also give you the more email-related stance: Respond to the emails you can, archive those which might come in handy, delete and unsubscribe those which are useless, and send your attachments to the cloud. In short, you just really have to sort out your inbox. While if you have a lot of mail traffic running your way and are afraid that it would disturb your progress, you can stuff all the old stuff into a folder for later and still keep up with your more recent day-to-day.

Therefore, start by looking at your schedule and opening up some space. Catch up on all the messages and conversations that clogged up your mail over time. Then, just take it by the hour until everything is sorted out.

When the Break Is Over

Once you have mopped, dusted, and taken back control over your inbox, you have to move your gaze to the future to prevent an overload from happening again. The best way would be to stay prepared and set yourself up for success by putting in that ounce of extra work.

First and foremost, it is crucial to understand how you use emails, your difficulties, and what strategies might work for you in the long run. This way, you can build a system that works for you and your way of life while keeping you in check and on the right side of the road. You can split yourself into three types of people when it comes to how you use emails: Those who respond immediately, those who respond quickly but never press delete, and then those who simply never read, reply or delete emails.

Let's say, for example, you are the latter. You would find it hard to keep track of your inbox once the book's dust has settled, and before you know it, you are right back where you started. You will need some strategies to help you get through the junk and remind you to keep things neat. Perhaps, setting reminders on your calendar would help? You could also create folders and set up rules that can give you an automated way of sorting out your emails without you having to pull too much weight on your shoulders. It is all about fitting your tactics to your person and what works best for you. Since you know you best, you must take it from here. Yet, I will as always, throw some incentives and ideas your way.

Take your time to sort through and handle your emails every day. Pick a time that suits you best. However, ensure that it does not take up most of your day and that you still have some time to play when you get home and on the weekends. Treat it as a short five-minute meeting between you and your emails; you could even note it on your calendar. I, for example, do enjoy multitasking. So, whenever I have my lunch, I take the time to sort my emails, arrange meetings, and respond to proposals. It is not something that will work for everyone, as lunch is sometimes the only time we get to catch a breath. It is simply something I have found that fits right into my system. Hence, you just have to find your very own version of a "lunch break" that helps you balance your life, even if it is only by a bit.

Another example of this would be to get intelligent and efficient in the way you work and spend your time toiling with emails. You want to work through them quickly, that much I know, and now that you have slapped a time frame onto the screen, it becomes even more actual. When your messages are vague or packed with words, the chances of a short email turning into a whole book of conversations and ex-planations are immense. Thus, why not keep things straightforward with better responses by writing briefer, sleeker emails that leave no room for misunderstandings? You can compile templates and canned responses where possible to up the speed at which you handle emails. You could even help yourself with specific apps and add-ons to help you transfer your emails from long and murky works to apparent forms of communication.

While you can move your way of communicating away from just emails. Although, it will not help you with your overall internet addiction. Still, if you have a problem with the clutter emails bring your way, you can move toward other means of communication, such as calling and internal tools, such as certain chat apps, while the best of them all would be to see your clients and people face-to-face.

All that is left for your prep is to take in your surroundings. Do this when you are working and when you take a look at your emails. Then work from there, using what you know and what works best for you to form a better, improved routine where your email has no hold over you. Incentives and techniques: That is all there is to it!

Disconnected From Mail Server

Finally, it is time to get to your break! This is when you should focus on yourself and everything that has nothing to do with your emails. What better place to start than setting up your plans and turning off notifications?

As you start your journey toward your occasional email leave, try and set up small changes and precautions to keep your mind at ease before you go offline from the mail servers. Set up automatic replies to let people trying to reach you know that you will get back to them in a while. You could even set one up for when you log off at work and for the weekends. That way, people will know that you are unavailable at those times and that you will be back in business in no time! It is about setting boundaries for yourself and others and finding ways to stick to them.

Detoxing from emails is not just about logging out of your account for a day or two. We do not want to miss out on things, remember? Work and pleasure included. Therefore, you will find that it turns out to be much more complicated than you think. It is an addiction, after all. Not something you can archive from time to time. You have to stay committed, get your support in order, and become that change you want to see yourself. So, if you think you have a better shot of removing yourself from your emails while dozing off on a good cocktail in the Maldives, why not book those tickets and put in your leave?

Chapter 8:

I'll Like All Your Posts

Even when you know that you have a problem with the internet, knowing whether your hardship lies with social media is another thing. Fortunately, the thing about having a social media addiction is that it is somewhat easy to identify and notice once you open your eyes to the crisis standing in front of you, which can show itself on various platforms such as Facebook, Twitter, and Instagram. You just have to remove those goggles framed with likes, shares, and views, as it is the only way to see what social media is genuinely doing to you.

The tells of a social media addiction are very similar to an internet addiction, which we touched on earlier (such as spending your hours online and not with your friends and family). We often feel the added social pressures of wanting to fit in with the crowd, compete with others and compare ourselves with their posts and profiles. We want to be online and exist with "relevancy" or whatever jargon you want to use. We all want to belong somewhere, so we live for our socials; however, that is where we went wrong.

Some people would do anything for a like. This act puts you at risk for dangerous behaviors, exacerbating symptoms of anxiety and depression, problems falling asleep, being distracted while awake, and having no time to spare when it comes to self-reflection and taking time for yourself. It consumes your life and stuffs you into penny-plain bios, profile pictures, and those limited reactions to posts. The question remains, as it does with a general internet obsession, whether or not you accept that you have a problem on your hands. Only then can you take that one step forward toward change.

Rather than trying to understand everything at once, why don't we start by asking ourselves a few simple questions to build some knowledge of ourselves and our use of social media:

- Have you melded social media into your day-to-day life? Must you use at least one platform as a custom throughout your day?

- Does your mood depend on social media? Is it your way of attaining excitement and happiness in your day?

- Do you find yourself using social media more and more, striving to get some kind of "buzz" or feeling of peace?

- Has your use of social media caused you any trouble? Are there conflicts between you and your loved ones? Or are you distracted and unproductive while at work?

- Are you nervous or feel unfulfilled whenever you take some time away from social media? Whether it be willingly or unwillingly.

- Have you tried stepping back from your platforms, or at least cutting back on the time you spend on them, but it either did not last very long, or you have moved the "start day" every time your planned date came along?

- While you are out and about (with others or alone), do you find yourself getting lost and distracted with the thoughts of what a great "post" or "profile picture" that moment would make? Do you spend more time updating and adding it to your wall or feed than you do living in the moment and being present?

- When scrolling through social media, do you feel gloomy, disgruntled, or as if you are not "good enough" because you did not get as many likes on your posts and pictures? This is especially true when you see how many likes, shares, and follows someone else gets.

- Do you feel better about who you are or have some sense of accomplishment and approval from others when you receive likes and flattering comments?

- Do you jump up or leave everything whenever you hear that notification sound go off? Are you hoping it is a like, share, comment, follow, or direct message? How do you feel when it is not one of those actions mentioned above (like some sort of google notification or your service provider telling you that you are running out of data)? Do you wait for a ring, buzz, or vibrate when your phone is quiet? How does it make you feel when no one reaches out to you or your socials turn mute?

Think before you answer these questions, answer them truthfully, and above all else, confront the problem if these questions, or most of them, apply to you. It can be hard to know whether you have a problem with using social media since it has become such a norm in our lives. It is a simple icon on our phones and devices that, with a simple tap, we can go into without even having to log in. Sometimes, we do not notice when we go into Facebook, when we view Instagram posts, and when a new tweet has found its way in front of us. It has become almost habitual and automatic. Admitting to having a problem is the first step, as they say, which is true. From there, you are responsible for focusing on what you are doing. Focus on why you are doing it and how you can remove your dependency from the posts and all the other muck. Old habits die hard; that is a fact, but habits are made to be broken and reshaped. They are not mechanical; they are mannerisms.

How to Cope With Post Overload

I will not lie; there is not really a thing like "post overload" per se, or it has not been copyrighted. I stole it from our previous chapter on emails if I am honest. Regardless, that is not paramount or relevant in this case. Our objectives are to find foolproof coping strategies to get us away from the post overload, or whatever you want to call it.

Ditching your life on social media might be especially hard for some since they need to "keep up with appearances" and keep their followers in the loop of what is going on in their lives. Your followers can wait. However, if it is really that essential to you, simply send out one of your posts and tell your followers that you need a much-needed "break" and that you will be off the radar for some time but that they can catch you once you are back.

If this is either essential for you to do, or you feel that you cannot go cold turkey on your people, do this as soon as you have set a date for when you will be M.I.A from your profile. Once you have taken care of your online reputation and follower follow-ups, you only have one more thing standing in your way: You. As I have said before, we often make these grandiose plans on how we will detox from our socials and take some time off in the real world, but without prevailing. I understand this completely, do not get me wrong. Spend half a day with me while I talk about going on yet another diet, and you will see just how hesitant I can be, especially when worrying about how it will look if I fail at another fad. But that's just it: Stepping past the fear of what others think is the first step in committing to your plans and having a form of accountability net to hold you to your word.

Still, sometimes even accountability is not enough to push you past yourself and all the excuses we tend to make for dropping our goals. *One bite will not hurt*, for example, is one of my favorites. Therefore, as with most things in life, your strongest competitor lies with your harshest critic and opponent—yourself. But that is why we set up strategies and learn tips before we sprint with ideas, such as a detox so that we know it will be harder for us to run ourselves down. That is precisely what we have here: Ways to ensure you do not get in your own way.

The best place to start is with those pesky things that keep us awake and demand our attention continuously: Notifications. If someone were to sit next to you, constantly poking and pinching at you to check your phone, you would do it, wouldn't you? Sure, you might end up screaming at them and clawing at their face, but you would still check it. Your notifications are the same, but we tend not to shush or push those away.

In truth, however, they are nothing more than distractions that make it merely impossible for you to keep up with your tasks and goals, especially when you are trying to get away from them. When you deliberately pull yourself away from social media, you will likely check up on them. Call it a pain or a test of self-will, but it gets especially hard. Therefore, when we scratch out the temptations, we are more likely to take control back over our focus and time.

If all else fails and you still find yourself drawn to your apps and unconsciously opening them up, your best bet would be to delete the apps from your devices altogether. A simple, quick uninstall, that is all. To begin with, you do not have to deactivate your account entirely and remove all the traces you ever had an account. The account can stay (if that is what you want). Just remove it from your devices. That is, if you can remember your login details. If you don't, it is not the end of the world; you can simply keep it on a device, like your laptop, that you use less than, for example, your smartphone. You can also hide them away in folders. That way, you still have some access to your profiles and accounts, but not as direct and handy as that simple click on your smartphone.

Last and worst-case scenario, why not pull out the plug on your internet? Disconnecting yourself from the internet means you cannot access it, and when you cannot use it, you will have no problem staying away from your social media. You could even switch off your device, which would keep you from getting online and take some time away from the real world.

Once you have taken care of the devices and apps, it is time to remove yourself even more from their allure. Action is the leading difference between success and falling back to old patterns. Hence, when you take action by stepping outside and away from social media, you will find that the detox runs a lot smoother than being stuck in the same room as Ms. TikTok.

The whole point of detoxing from social media (and the internet in general, for that matter) is about trekking back into the real world and taking back everything the plugs have snatched away. Is there any better way of doing this than meeting with people? It goes without saying that I am definitely not talking about virtual meetings either.

Once you are out of your profile, it is time to set up a date with all those friends and followers you have. Meet up for a coffee, regroup for an exercise class, or simply sit down for a good ol' talk. Why not go crazy and join a club or two and meet strangers?

I know that making friends and getting back to mingling might come off as a startling and frustrating plan. Regardless, it cannot hurt to try. You might even find that fraternizing, making friends, and reconnecting with others are much better than doing it online. Just be sure not to drop a like at everything they say or leave a snarky remark whenever your opinions are not the same.

You could also take a moment to sit with your family and loved ones to hear them out on their point of view and how your social media addiction has affected them. Explain to them that you are turning over a new leaf and taking on a fresh start without social media toppling it all. Tell them about this book and everything you have learned, the steps you plan to take, and how you plan to become a better, more present person. As well as motivating and holding you accountable, it allows you to reconnect with them and strengthen your relationship.

Last but certainly not least, seek a social connection while putting your good foot forward and helping others. Yes, you heard me, head out and volunteer. Besides enriching your community, you will also stand up for things that matter to you. Gratitude and happiness will flood your way (and toward others). It is something that social media simply cannot hold a candle to! You might even pick up a friend or two while you are there.

Then, as you know, you still have to take care of *numero uno*. We often find ourselves stuck and caught up in the "what ifs" and "if only" that tomorrow brings. We know that it often prevents us from making the best of our present and every memory along the way. However, there is another thing your addiction to social media has corrupted. Your ability to look inside and glimpse your needs is affected. Let me ask you this: When was the last time you took care of yourself?

Loving yourself is a one-way ticket to conquering your voyage of detoxing. When you and your mind are clear, loved, and happy, it is solely a recipe for a strong foundation that keeps giving!

So, why not take your time away from all things digital to focus on being mindful, showing gratitude, reflecting, and showing yourself some self-love? I know you might be thinking, *who has the time and money for that? What does this have to do with a digital or social media detox anyway?*

To begin with, you have some spare time on your hands since you are no longer throwing it all into your digital upkeep. As for money, you do not have to spend thousands of dollars on expensive spa treatments, isolated holidays, or extreme spending sprees (unless that is what you want, of course). Self-care can be as simple as taking a walk outside, telling yourself how good you look with a finger gun in the mirror, or drinking a nice cup of tea. You do not need to spend a dime.

While self-care, loving yourself, being mindful, grateful, and venting has everything to do with ditching your tech. Addiction most often takes a toll on your mental health and general well-being. All your techniques of looking after yourself, especially without any digital distractions, are ways in which you can live presently and sweeten your mental well-being. It is not just a distraction from social media; it is a way for you to get better.

Calling It Quits

Sometimes, when all the detox is behind you, you find that you were better off from the start and that maybe it is time to cut the cord on the whole ordeal. Yes, I know, *quitting social media forever?! Who would do such a thing?!* You would be surprised to find out how many people resign from social media. In the US, for example, a whopping 45% of users have logged off permanently, and that is only the stats for Facebook (Statista, 2022).

The book is not strived to force you into giving up your digital life, going off the grid, and running wild with the sheep along the mountain ridges. You do not have to throw all your apps and accounts into the bin if that is not what you want. There is still some catching up to do and some detoxing. Perhaps, in the end, you might see things a bit differently. So, just in case that happens, here are some ways to make the detox more permanent (or at least make yourself less dependent).

If, after your detox, you are still unsure whether or not to break social media off from your life, try and keep some space and constraints for the time being. You have to make changes to your lifestyle and digital etiquette, and it all starts with tracking.

By this, I mean literally keeping a stern eye on the amount of time you spend on all your social media platforms. Then, at the end of the day, add up all your overall times. It could be 10 minutes on Instagram, 15 on Facebook, 20 minutes on YouTube, and 5 on Tumblr (which would add up to about 50 minutes across-the-board). Once you know how much of your day you spend lost in the posts, you have control over whether you want to cut back on those minutes.

You could set up times and reminders for when you want to shut down your phone (and block out the digital world) when you will plug out the internet, and when you will keep your phone away for good, like a good hour or two before bed. It is about striking a balance in your life and setting boundaries. That way, your detox will not be for nothing, and you will not be stuck in a vicious cycle of detox, post-overload, and repeat.

Before It's Over

Now, to get with the program and help those of you who want to say your forever farewells, here are some ways you can do just that:

- Create that final post for old-time's sake. Say your final good-byes when you throw your dramatic exit (or subtle one). Pack your bags full of all the essential things you have left on your wall before you finally shut the social media door behind you and hit the road. It can give you that final closure before leaving that digital space behind while giving you some sense of accountability because no one wants to face the awkwardness of an on-and-off relationship.

- Find a new plaything or hobby to replace the free time you have opened for yourself. Try new things or take up something you have not done in a long time. When it comes to finding something you enjoy doing, you never know which one you could end up making your own. I, for one, never dreamed of kicking up my ability to play the recorder! Regardless, I did leave it after some time for another habit. Still, never shut yourself down to the endless possibilities the world and all we have created have to offer.

- Treat and praise yourself for quitting and all the smaller milestones you will make along the way. Save up for a weekend away and take it, all because you went a few weeks without worrying about what Sandy had to say about the latest celeb gossip or what Daniel had for lunch. (Which, I know, are terrible examples of social media use).

- Always keep the benefits close to you and remind yourself what drove you to social media in the first place and why you wanted out. Leave yourself incentives wherever you can: Try a motivational lock screen, some stickers on your phone cover, even a simple paper slapped onto your wall reading, *"Social media is no good for you,"* will suffice. Do not let your hard work be for nothing. It will not always be easy, of course. You just have to keep at it, stay motivated, and keep going strong.

- If all of the fake news has not convinced you yet, you should know that you should not be getting all your information from social media. Go out and find some other sources instead. Staying in touch with current events can be as simple as subscribing to newsletters, and RSS feeds from the news sources you enjoy reading. You could also just turn on the TV and keep up with the news. While if you find yourself feeling a bit nostalgic or retro or just want something more tech-free, you could always pick up a trusted magazine or newspaper.

- If you know that one of your friends or family members also wants to click on that 'Delete Account' button, why not ask them whether you can make it a team effort? Working with someone else towards a common goal can be a great way of locking in some motivation and support. You could also look around for some online communities and support groups for internet addiction. It is a way of throwing that extra pep in your step, which helps you commit for the long run while making friends.

Furthermore, the best you can do is embrace the present with open arms and take care of yourself and others, all while taking advantage of your new-found free time.

Never go cold-turkey straight out of the gate. You will have withdrawal symptoms when you try to get away from bad habits or stop an addiction. They are ruthless in the process's first few days, weeks, and sometimes months. It also means you have a greater risk of falling short of your goals, giving up on them altogether, and giving in to the temptations around you. Therefore, preparing yourself for the quits by detoxing and dropping the impact of social media in your life is essential. A stitch in time saves nine, as they say. All of these parts work together. Preparation is vital, and while these strategies and tips will only get you halfway, the rest is all up to you!

Chapter 9:

The Wide World That Webs

———●———

We already defined the compulsive use of the internet and technology as putting an extensive amount of time and effort into your on-screen activities. It becomes ingrained into our minds—a habit we surely lean on. We become bound to it, and when our batteries are low, and we are offline, everything comes tumbling down, or at least that is how it feels to us.

The internet and our devices are not all about checking your emails and using social media; there is an assortment of things left for you to do. That is the glory of it. Because of this, so many of us fall into the snares of addiction so easily. We enjoy the dopamine hit we get from these activities way too much just to give it up, but that is precisely when we have to call it quits; before it is too late and the buttons and keys are all we can see.

Still, as the definition implies, it is nothing more than an addiction, and addictions can be broken, and their damages can be reversed. You just have to understand how their gears turn and how the mechanisms grow. This, simply put, is about addressing how severely your addiction holds onto you and how you can clip your ties with it once and for all.

How Strong Is Its Grip?

The *compulsive internet use scale* allows for evaluating the severity of internet addiction, compulsive behavior, and pathological online behavior (Milasauskiene et al., 2021). The DSM-IV criteria were used in the development of this instrument, and even though it might seem like a quick and easy test to run through, it has proven to be a unique way of working out how much baggage you will need to shake.

I believe we have already discussed the criteria within the definition of digital addiction in the first chapter. These criteria such as endangering your relationships with those around you, all for the thrill of a click. Therefore, we do not have to run through it again; I just thought you would have wanted to know a bit of background on the test before you get to it.

Measuring Weights

Below you will find the compulsive internet use scale, which we will use to address the stringency of your internet addiction and to determine how much work and strategies you will need to implement to improve and show the digital world who is boss. So, why don't I tell you how this is going to work?

The questions you will scale were all pulled out with the five symptoms of addiction: Loss of control, withdrawal, mood modifications, preoccupation, and conflict. All you have to do is answer these questions truthfully by highlighting or circling the number that you feel fits with your lifestyle and ways. The numbering works like this:

1. Never

2. Rarely

3. Sometimes

4. Often

5. Regularly

For now, you do not have to worry about doing anything with these numbers. Just focus on answering the questions, and we will get to what you have to do after and how you can sketch out the results once you are done.

Take your time running through these questions, and do not settle for a number unless you are sure it is true to you and your circumstances. Remember that it does not help to try and make yourself "look good" or lie to yourself. You know who you are and what you are going through, and even when you might be your harshest critic, do not judge! Do not forget that you are here trying to help yourself (and your loved ones) strive towards a better, less digital life. Being honest, in all honesty, is the only way you will be able to do just that. So, I guess all that I have to ask before you can go on your way is: *How often?*

- Do you find it hard to pull away from the Internet when you are using it?

1	2	3	4	5

- Do you continue to use the Internet despite trying to stop?

1	2	3	4	5

- Do others complain about your Internet use or suggest that you spend less time online?

1	2	3	4	5

- Do you stay awake because of the Internet?

1	2	3	4	5

- Do you think about the Internet or tech when you are not using it?

1	2	3	4	5

- Do you prefer being online and in front of a screen instead of spending time with others?

1	2	3	4	5

- Do you think you should use your Internet and tech less?

1	2	3	4	5

- Do you think you should spend less time on the Internet and on your devices?

1	2	3	4	5

- Have you tried to reduce your digital time, but without success?

1	2	3	4	5

- Do you rush through your work to go onto the Internet or do something else on your devices?

1	2	3	4	5

- Do you neglect other obligations in your life for some time on the Internet and on your devices?

1	2	3	4	5

- Do you go onto the Internet when you are feeling down, anxious, and not quite like yourself?

1	2	3	4	5

- Do you use the Internet and tech as an escape route from negative feelings and problems in your real life?

1	2	3	4	5

- Do you feel restless, frustrated, or irritated when you cannot use the Internet?

1	2	3	4	5

Once you are done, and you are happy with your answers, snatch a piece of paper or use your head and add up all the individual numbers. If you did not *catch my drift*, you would have a mark counting out 70. If you are anywhere near that total, you know that your addiction has reached a severe high, while anything from 35 and up means you have a problem that might become bitter if you let it stand over time. You could also try counting how many occurrences you have of each number. If you primarily chose ones, then you might be well off. But, at the same time, the intensity of your addiction increases if the majority of your choices are higher on the scale.

The results will guide you in understanding that, even when you do not want to admit it, you have a serious problem that is critical to address. Even if your number is not high, if you have a problem, it is better to hit it on the head than waiting for it to grow in your life. However, if your results were a bit worse than you would have liked them to be, then you might have to implement more strategies and changes in your life to remove the root of the addiction. It is not a solid fate; people are different, so what I am saying now can be entirely different for some. Still, at least now you know what part the internet plays in your life. Regardless, one question (which was not a part of the scaling test) stands in importance above all else: *Why did you decide to make the change?*

Cutting Cords

We live in an age dominated by technology; sometimes, escaping it seems improbable. However, it is not impossible. When you open your eyes to your dependencies and truly focus on how present technology is, you can quickly start reshaping your routines and detoxing from the blue lights in your life._

I will not lie, and I know that saying this is not traditional, but most of this chapter was already covered in previous chapters, primarily within chapter six. Therefore, things here will be short and sweet, and I do advise you to go back and review the last chapters, as it would not hurt!

First and foremost, the best thing you can do is to take the time to remove any tech distractions from your environment while keeping yourself occupied with more tech-free solutions. That way, the temptations are not in your way, and your chance of not pressing that "on" button is much greater. You have to point down your focus and attention to that which is essential so that you can stay on track and hold up to the promises you have made to yourself.

Your strategies to hold away the internet and devices are your best shot to get what you want, along with a sturdy look on your mental health and a network of support to hold you up when you are down.

However, I think it would be best to pull apart the reasons why we use technologies and look at them as they stand on their own.

Looking Up Too Much

The world wide web is a very spacious place, as you know. There are thousands of sources and pieces you can go through. Information is everywhere and anywhere at all times. It is no surprise why it can often become so overwhelming. If you remember, I mentioned this scenario before; it is commonly known as 'information overload.'

Information overload is precisely how it sounds: Overloading yourself with information until you cannot hold on to the freight anymore. After all, your brain is just like a dump truck, and when you throw too much sand into its box, it simply will not work the way it should. You have to know your gross vehicle weight.

The overload itself can come in many shapes and sizes. It could constantly be looking things up every chance you get, such as when someone, or even you, have a question or you just want to add some spice to your conversations by dropping in an interesting fact or two. Perhaps you just want to research some things repeatedly, even if the topic remains the same. Then there is the snare of constant gossip, articles, websites, reading, learning, and browsing through pieces of information, which often leads to the glut we are often struck by.

The best possible action would be to restrict yourself from those things that are taking up your mind and piling up against you. You could, for example, restrict some of the sites you usually visit and use other apps, settings, and software that can limit your internet access and general tech use.

Try to keep things as personalized as possible so that you can keep things tidy, separate, and limited as much as possible. You need to have balance, especially if you work with technology. You do not want to distract yourself with all the information you love to look at, but you also want your job. Therefore, the best way to do this would be to limit access to that you do not need, stick with what you are busy with, hold onto your obligations, and kick away all those unrelated tasks. You can do this for the internet, some of your devices, or both, if you feel it would be best.

Furthermore, as a way of tracking yourself and ensuring that you do not subconsciously browse, set up small "check-ups" for yourself. You could either choose to redirect your focus every now and again, but I do find that it can be a hard thing to do. I have found that setting reminders throughout the day helps snip you out of any possible informational binges. You could either set it up on your devices while you attend to your work, or you can use other "reminding devices" such as electronic timers, alarm clocks, watches, and even egg timers will do! It is just a way of regularly popping in to see how you are holding up with the detox, what struggles you have, the withdrawal symptoms you are undergoing, how you are feeling, your victories, and that whole lot.

Moreover, your basic guidelines for a digital detox, such as getting out of the house and away from your tech, will do you wonders.

Playing Outside

Using technology and the internet for our own entertainment is possibly the most relatable and well-known reason that we use them in the first place. However, it is also the primary reason why so many of us become addicted.

We turn over in bed with the TV blaring in the background. We always carry our phones on the side of our hips, that is, if it is not glued to our ears. Our thumbs are quite the buff digits from all those video games.

We often rely on our devices to make us feel happy, fulfilled, and amused. I cannot tell you how many times I have heard, "*I cannot go without my phone,*" or, "*I cannot imagine how people lived without the internet back in the day!*" It is simple; people were people like you and me, but they lived in the outside world without the digital barrier that has split many of us away from others and the opportunity to live our lives to their fullest! However, the good news is that it would be never too late to turn in our phones and take a step out.

You just have to find a way of disconnecting that works for you and keeps you entertained, such as taking up scrapbooking (which, I know, is a cliché). Get creative, experiment with various things, and fall back into activities you know you love. The choice is entirely up to you! Yet, I did compile some activities for you to look at. Call it inspiration or consideration. Regardless, why not give some of them a go?

- Hit the kitchen and try cooking up some new recipes.

- You can bake cookies (or any other dessert you like or want to try).

- Stack up a bonfire outside and roast a couple of marshmallows.

- Wrap up some sweetmeats and goodies before throwing them into a basket and taking the family out for a picnic.

- Throw the flour out and make a pizza from scratch, and if that is not your cup of tea, try making doughnuts, pretzels, or anything else.

- Go for a walk, run, hike, or bike ride (it is up to you).

- Play frisbee in the park (you do not have to be so specific), or take your dog for an outing.

- Shoot some hoops, play a game of hockey, soccer, or any other sport of choice.

- Dive in for a swim at the beach, build a sandcastle, or put together a treasure hunt.

- Meet up with some friends or go see your relatives (why not take a look at those old family albums?)

- Challenge someone in a board game like Scrabble, Monopoly, Cluedo, or a simple chess game.

- Get creative and take on an art or DIY project.

- Pull together a time capsule and bury it somewhere in the yard.

- Grab some garbage bags and clean up around the neighborhood (you can even go ahead and plant a tree somewhere).

- Tend to your garden, plant some new flowers, fertilize the soil, and hang up a birdhouse or bird feeder.

- Clean up around the house (keep some old things in boxes to donate to your local thrift shop or donation drop-off).

As you can see, you can literally do almost anything to keep yourself and your mind busy and away from the temptation of digital entertainment. My friend, for example, even took on cutting up birthday balloons to make dresses for his daughter's dolls. Anything goes around here!

Free From Automation

Almost everything we use in our daily lives is automatic. The only difference is we barely recognize or acknowledge their presence these days because they have just always been around these days.

I will not lie. Most of these automation appliances, such as your car or your washing machine, are pretty harmless due to digital addiction. Just because I have not met anyone addicted to washing their laundry does not mean you cannot get addicted to more inactive technologies.

However, I have added this here simply because it cannot hurt to detox from all forms of electronics. You do not have to skip your daily coffee and toast, but why not try and go through the day without using the escalator? Walk to work or grab your bike before heading out to the shops. Chop and peel your own veggies and fruits this time around. It is all about grabbing back your dependency and learning to live more freely. So, why not go all in?!

Professional Outreach

Throughout the book, I have called upon you to reach out to your family members and friends while assembling a few new ones along the way. Call me a wingman, encourager, or whatever you like, but I still stand by my viewpoint.

However, one more fiber in your security net that you should hear about: The professional one. Many people feel ashamed to seek help, fearing they may come across as weak. Nonetheless, there is no reason whatsoever for you to feel this way. Addiction caresses itself in different forms for everyone, and not all of us can deal with it alone or with these strategies independently. Therefore, if you ever feel you need that extra pint of help during your journey, reach out.

You can start seeing a therapist, join a support group, call a hotline, or even if you feel that it is what you need, book yourself into rehab. There is no shame in getting better—always remember that.

Looking After You

Remember that this thing that has its hold on you is nothing more than some digital and material something in your life. Believe it or not, you will not die without these gadgets and connected statuses in your life. Think about it: Humans were more than fine going without all the smartphones, computers, doodads, and doohickeys once. So, why not go back in time and take on their ways?

Then again, it is harder said than done, as most of us have grown up with these conveniences by our side. Perhaps, it is just that we do not know any better. We have accepted technologies as our familiarities, and they are not going anywhere anytime soon. Regardless, that does not make us incapable of slimming down on how, when, and how often we use these luxuries. However, the responsibility to take action is yours alone. No one else can take that step for you.

A study from NordVPN showed that, on average, we could spend up to and over 27 years online throughout our lives (Higgins, 2021). That is an entire adult! You could have taken 160 tours to the moon or Mount Everest in the time you have spent connected. You could run over 10 000 marathons, walk the Great Wall of China 17 and a half times, and watch the entire The Simpsons series over a thousand times (which, in all honesty, probably would just have fueled the fire, though).

Think about those statistics and how serious they are. Technology and the need to be online steals a great deal of time from your life. Do you really think it is worth it? I don't.

If you were just to take a step away from the screen, you would see a whole life waiting for you on the other side—your life. Do not throw it away for something as simple as a Wi-Fi hotspot! Think about how fast the past ten years have gone by. On average, we live up to 75 years of age. It is no more than a blink of an eye! Before you know it, your battery has run up.

You have a limited time in this world and with those you love, and if that is not enough to convince you, I don't know what can. The best billboard sign, wake-up call, and piece of advice I can give you are to ditch the tech and go out and live your life the way you should have!

STEP THREE:
SELF-CARE FOLLOW THROUGH WITH AFTERCARE

Chapter 10:

Keeping Yourself Up

Once you have made it, you have made it! And I would like to congratulate you on making it this far (even if you have not done it yet and were planning on starting once you have finished this read). Whatever the scenario might be, *salute*!

Once the detox is over, you still have some ground to cover, though. After that, you are, to some degree, home free! However, for now, as I just said, we still have some sentences to read and things to do. This section is all about holding your side of the cable management and dust collectors clean and keeping it that way by making permanent changes in your life and behaviors that will make you a better "user" in the real world. This is the basics of following through with your aftercare and ensuring that you hit the grand slam.

The reablement, just like in hospitals, is aimed to get you adjusted to your condition; about learning new skills that you need every day and making something possible, such as less dependency on the internet. In this case, it is about whetting you for after the detox and ensuring that you do not go back to your old ways simply because we do not want that!

Sticking With Schedules

Schedules are how we jot down and plan our days while identifying the time, order, and priority of tasks and operations. When we wake up, we first run our day through our minds: We think about all of the things we have to do that day, what we want to do first, how much time we want to allocate to specific tasks, how long our lunch break will be, and all those bits and pieces. When we write out our schedules, we are essentially finding ways to work and communicate these thoughts into something more physical.

We know that to truly grasp and hold onto the advantages of digital detox and its aftermath, we have to change the way we think and do things, or, in short, we should look at our behaviors. Our manners are like these lumpy orbs that are made up of routines, which are made up of habits. Once we modify these two, we can create solid spheres.

One way we can do this is by setting up schedules. Now you might think routines and schedules are the same things. Yes, their similarities are almost familial, but still not quite hitting the same spot. Routines are all the steps needed to complete and knock off your program, while the schedule is a big picture of what will happen during the day. So, they are more like colleagues than they are cousins.

The point with all this is that your schedule is the very first step in taking on your mannerisms, habits, and overall routines, which you need to reshape to get a better hold on your life and digital ways.

A schedule gives your life the structure and discipline it needs to get you through all the uncertainties, stress, fatigue, and unhealthy patterns. A schedule is an anchor in your life that holds you down to everything necessary. It keeps you away from all the distractions at the top since all your attention and energy go into everything you do.

While since you are following a more straightforward and precise daily routine, you will also be conserving your time. No more time will be wasted on a messy do-this-do-that agenda and unproductive activities, such as getting stuck on the web. This could also mean you have some time to kill with spontaneity.

You will also be able to create more effective time blocks ("blocks" or periods you set aside for a particular task). This can help you fine-tune your time management skills and your day-to-day by allowing you to see where you can adjust your time, where you spend most of it, and where you can get some time put to the side in case of emergencies or free time. Just consider the time you have to thread in for your detox strategies.

On the mention of "emergencies" and related things, I thought it would also be essential to bring up how important it is to prepare for a stormy day. Perhaps you have one off-days where you are met with more temptations you can handle, and you need to take a few minutes to catch a breather. When you keep a space open in your schedule, you can help yourself get out of a rut. While you are generally in a better place to deal with any other problems and pop-ups that might occur, such as a surprise meeting or personal problems. This is just a way to ensure that even fewer factors can throw your schedule off course.

It is also a great way to solidify plans with everyone, whether your boss or family members. You can keep them in the loop on your goals, how you are progressing, and when you have some time to spend with them. It is also a great, low-key way of reestablishing, strengthening, and protecting your boundaries and sharing them with others.

Schedules are just great tools that can provide us with productive, meaningful days that inspire and motivate while giving us that boost of accomplishment and confidence we need.

While above all else, it gives us time. We need something to spend on things that matter the most to us. It can be your own booklet on getting things under control and beneath your hold.

The How To

Setting up your schedule is easy once you have gotten the hang of it and learned to flow with all the ins and outs. Still, I will give you a quick setup guide and sample to get you started before you take it all into your own hands and fill in your very own that applies to your own life.

So, here are some steps you can take to get started:

- Write out a sloppy list of all your tasks. They do not have to be in a cohesive order or anything. Just write them down, so you have them in front of you. Sometimes, it helps to throw all the puzzle pieces onto the table before you start piecing them together.

- Remember to include everything you do during the day, even when they might not seem like your traditional activities, such as your meal times, sleep times, and breaks. Work on your strategies, such as taking a walk during lunch. Even though your detox is over, be sure to add your tech times, including that sneaky five minutes on social media you slid into your day.

Additionally, set aside time for you to be alone and do things that make you feel better and lower your stress levels.

- When you are done, you can underline, star, or mark the most important tasks and those who take up the most of your time. Use different marks as you move down on your priorities, or simply number them down.

- Take your energy and productivity in mind before allocating time to each task you have. You can take an evaluation time to see how you handle individual tasks and how much time you need when busy with certain things. Once you have a general summary and have figured things out a bit more, you can adjust and fix your times as needed.

- Bad habits need no invitation; therefore, set up reminders to ensure that you are still sticking with your tasks and priorities, or you can use any other sort of reminder and fail-safe you prefer.

- Build a schedule that works for you and makes you excited to start your day. You could set up multiple ones for different reasons (daily schedule, bullet journal, goal prioritization, weekly schedule). After that, you can start filling out your tasks in their appropriate places and making the schedule your own.

In With the Samples

So, pretend I have just scribbled down a handwritten schedule and plopped it down for you below. However, I should warn you that it is a bit sloppy, but I wanted to get in as much variety as I could:

Date: 7 September 2022

Strategies for the Day:

- Take breaks to move away from the tech

- Go out for lunch with mom

- Keep the phone away from the bedroom

- Set physical alarm for tomorrow morning

- Draw before bed

Daily Goals:

- Do not spend time on the internet or devices while at home (I get enough tech time at work)

- Draw a bit before bed

- Spend time with my loved ones

TO-DO LIST

05:00	☐	Get ready for the day (dress up, grab a water, etc.)
06:00	☐	Exercise
07:00	☐	Have a nutritional breakfast
08:00	☐	Call some clients (especially Mrs. Stone) using the office landline
09:45	☐	Take a good look at the accounts (those on paper)
10:00	☐	Stretch out, take a walk around the office, or sort some things out
11:00	☐	Run through some projects and make adjustments where needed
12:00	☐	Call clients for meeting confirmations (use some post-its to keep notes, and jot down important dates onto schedule)
12: 30	☐	Take a break and look around me (take in the surroundings, while using all my senses)
12:55	☐	Pack up all the tech and stack some paper on desk for later
13:00	☐	Meet mom for lunch date
14:00	☐	Do some research and start writing speech for upcoming seminar (use the books I got from the library and the paper on my desk)
16:00	☐	Log out from all devices, pack up my stuff, and log off at work
17:00	☐	Grab the cookbook, prepare dinner, and give the dog his dinner as well before we all sit down to eat
19:00	☐	Take a relaxing bath and start prepping for bed (but really give myself a pamper to destress)
19:58	☐	Plug phone in the living room to recharge for tomorrow
20:00	☐	Grab a notebook and some pencils and jump into bed
20:45	☐	Turn off all the lights, turn around, and try dozing off

Penny for My Thoughts:

Today was a good day, I think. I had temptations, of course, especially since my work demands working with tech and communicating with clients. However, I tried cutting down on the internet and devices whenever I could. I had a delightful lunch with mom as well. I had your usual Farmhouse option, with extra egg, while she had some kind of cereal. Dad says "hi" too. I did really well at home, and only checked my phone four times the whole night, which is a record! Before bed, I drew a bit. The drawing itself was no *Mona Lisa*, but still, I tried something new, and quite enjoyed it actually. Maybe tomorrow I can try knitting?

The Doodle Box

Mr. Donaldson—Meeting next week Monday at three

Bring along samples; proposals; business strategies; pamphlets;

Arrange for a table for two at Bonne Nourriture

Call Jacob and ask whether we can meet up later that day

So, there you have it! Your very own samples of a schedule. Furthermore, remember to stay focused and on the ball, to glance at your schedule as often as you can, and keep your life happy, good, balanced, and screen-free to the best of your abilities!

I am not saying that with schedules, you can plan and stick to all your goals, obligations, and tasks, but it is undoubtedly a place to start! So, what are you waiting for? Set one up yourself!

Habitual Turn Arounds

I have touched on habits previously; however, it would be fitting to discuss how you could change your patterns with the internet and devices to better handle your life and circumstances in the future.

I suggest we start by examining habits from the inside and out. They mainly consist of three parts: Reminder, routine, and reward. I have touched on the reminder and reward before, but I wanted to make it more exact.

The cue is one thing, whether it be a person, feeling, occurrence, or conscious behavior, that pushes and "triggers" you to do the habitual action. After some time, when the trigger and the act itself have been done quite a few times consecutively, the habit sticks in your mind and life and becomes a usual routine. While the reason why you keep on doing the same thing over and over again (even when you get the same results) is that you have associated some kind of reward with the habit..

All three of them work in a cycle, repeating themselves continuously time and time again until the pattern is disrupted, altered, put down, or enhanced. Leaving the digital world behind means doing all those things, and here is how you would do just that.

Triggers are the first part of creating a habit. Therefore, we must track our routines to identify any patterns and triggers that might pop up. It allows us to break old habits while strengthening the new action we associate with the said trigger.

With the internet, for example, if we tend to overindulge in online activities when we are nervous, we know that the uneasy feeling is what triggers and leads us to turn on our computers. To change the outcome of our routines, we should know what our triggers are to avoid what we usually do. Referring to the example, let's say you feel nervous because you have an important meeting coming up around the corner. Now, instead of going online, you step out and play some soccer. You do this every time you feel anxious. Sooner or later, you turn around, and you have replaced this set-in-mind routine with something better and healthier

You do not have to take up all your bad habits at once. If you spend too much time on social media, play too many hours of online gaming, and take way too many selfies, you can simply decide on one bad habit, set up little changes, and stick to your changed (and improved) routine from there on out until you have scratched out everything on your list.

You must visualize yourself breaking your habits, focusing on why you wanted to change first, loving yourself every step of the way, and giving it time, because nothing can happen overnight. While you should also try and stitch in ways to keep yourself motivated and punched on track, such as setting reminders, preparing for setbacks, and working on any issues you might have stuck at the root.

You have to accept that the process is not going to be an easy one-and-done thing. It will be challenging at times and easy as pie on other days. Do not settle for an all-or-nothing mindset because it just will not work. Accept that you will stumble, but that if you keep at it, you will not end up falling.

Last Words on Fast Detoxes

No matter how much we wish it could be otherwise, one detox will not do the trick. Therefore, you might have to throw in a couple during the year whenever you feel it is necessary. You know how to do a detox by now, which is excellent. However, you might also find it beneficial to go on digital fasts. This is basically, more or less, the same as a detox, except that you should stay away from tech and the internet at all times, even when you have some obligations. It can be fasting from six at night until the next morning, a whole day, or simply an hour or two every day. Therefore, it would be best to do this while you have the time to be away and without them, like when you are on vacation, have some time off, or on the weekends. It is almost like taking on an extra step of detox where the intensity is higher for some, and it is more regular and aimed at not cleansing your system from the digital world but keeping it clean.

Conclusion:

Before We Switch Off

There is a power in control that no one can take from us, not even the big bad wolf we know as the digital world. We are often lost in its grasp; sometimes, we stumble when trying to find our way out. It is the darndest thing; how something intended to be so good can leave everything we have in a complete mess.

However, that is just the thing: We do have a say in the matter. You can either decide to allow the internet and all the tech we get to control our lives or turn the cards and handle it instead.

I know that you might be scared to even start on this journey of cleansing yourself from all the plugs and startups, but it all starts with that one simple shuffle of courage. As the Chinese proverb says, "Be not afraid of growing slowly, be afraid only of standing still" (MacKay, 2019), and right now, my reader, you cannot afford to waver.

There is an entire world, full of those you love and have yet to meet, waiting for you to put down those headphones and close the screen on your online activities. All you have to do is take a step and commit to a better life.

You have the tools in the palm of your hands; you need to take the wheel, trust yourself, and use them every chance you get. You have learned what it means to have an internet addiction, what you are up against, what has kept you plugged in for so long, how you got here in the first place, and the causes, signs, and symptoms. You have a roadmap of self-management instruments that will lead you down the road of disaster recovery. This is where you can finally learn what it takes to beat your dependencies, shed your emails, log out from social media, and finally look after yourself when all your hard work is done.

Remember that this is not a sprint, a competition, or a one-and-done process. It is a constant effort you have to make and put in so you can have a better chance at life and what you truly deserve.

No matter what the strategies are and the advice I can give, you have to understand that the only way this can possibly work and turn out in your favor is when you give it your all and believe that you are capable of achieving greatness without the tech and internet holding your hand.

Live your life, my friend, and live it to its fullest extent while being present in the real world, with real people, and loving yourself for who you are with the screens turned black. Your life is worth so much more, and once you realize that, you have years to play with, memories to make, and loads of phones to break!

The thud of hitting the dirt knocked the wind out of me. For a moment, all I could hear was the shrieking whistle of a hummingbird sticking out of a tree somewhere. What a drop that was!

With a stifled laugh, I sat up, resting my arms on my knees and looking out at the scenery. At first, I had no idea what had happened. One minute I was running along the trail, and the next, I was thrown into a cloud of dust right onto my behind! It must have been a rock tucked under the grassy corners of the road. Now, here I was: On the ground.

I pulled myself up from the soil, dusting off the thin layer of sand that clung to my running shorts. Like an unfit ostrich, I stretched my aching legs, pulling thick thorns from the thread of my cotton shirt, leaving specks of blood to peek through the fabric. It stung. However, I guess my gallant endeavors to take control over my life and to boot tech and the internet to the side will keep me going through my pangs and the remaining miles. The pains and determination, it seems, go hand in hand with living life.

A deep frown cracked on my forehead as the sun beat down on my already dripping crown. Yet still, I remained on the path, firmly in place, assertive, and determined to get this walk over with. I cannot let the addiction win... No, let me rephrase that: I will not allow it to win, and today it was up to me to defeat my foe. It is not only a notable distraction but my road toward triumph.

I jerked myself forward with a wide grin, flying across the plains. I will not allow myself to be defeated by something as simple as gadgets and connectivity. No, not a chance!

References

Arden-Close, E., McAlaney, J., & Ali, R. (2019, July 2). *Digital addiction: how technology keeps us hooked.* The Conversation. https://theconversation.com/digital-addiction-how-technology-keeps-us-hooked-97499

Asano, E. (2017, January 4). *How much time do people spend on social media?* Social Media Today. https://www.socialmediatoday.com/marketing/how-much-time-do-people-spend-social-media-infographic

Autonomous. (2018, November 2). *What is email overload, and how can you avoid it?* Autonomous. https://www.autonomous.ai/ourblog/what-is-email-overload-and-how-can-you-avoid-it

Baylor University. (2016, October 20). *Are you addicted to social media? Experts offer six questions to ask yourself.* Media and Public Relations | Baylor University. https://www.baylor.edu/mediacommunications/news.php?action=story&story=174059

Bozoglan, B. (2019). *The Impact of family on digital addiction: An overview. Multifaceted Approach to Digital Addiction and Its Treatment.* https://www.igi-global.com/chapter/the-impact-of-family-on-digital-addiction/229190

Brooks, R. (2018, February 8). *How technology impacts sleep quality.* Aastweb.org. https://www.aastweb.org/blog/how-technology-impacts-sleep-quality

Cosslett, R. L. (2014, January 9). *Five ways to curb your internet use and get your life back.* The Guardian. https://www.theguardian.com/commentisfree/2014/jan/09/5-ways-internet-use-web-addiction

Cross, K. T. (2022). *Get Your Glow Back and Reclaim Your Energy: Daily Reminders to Inspire Healthy Living.* Independently published.

CUA Health Insurance. (n.d.). *How to plan and survive a digital detox.* Www.cua-health.com.au. https://www.cuahealth.com.au/guide/plan-survive-digital-detox

de Morree, P. (2019, April 24). *Email detox: Practical tips to cure the addiction.* Corporate Rebels. https://corporate-rebels.com/email-detox/

Dholakia, U. (2016, May 4). *What is a digital fast and should I go on one?* Www.psychologytoday.com. https://www.psychologytoday.com/us/blog/the-science-behind-behavior/201605/what-is-digital-fast-and-should-i-go-one

Elkatmis, B. (2020, August 18). *Spend a lot of time online? It may affect your sleep.* Sciworthy. https://sciworthy.com/spend-a-lot-of-time-online-it-may-affect-your-sleep/

Eyal, N. (2013, October 2). *How to break 5 soul-sucking technology habits.* Nir and Far. https://www.nirandfar.com/how-to-break-5-soul-sucking-technology-habits/

Gallo, A. (2012, February 21). *Stop email overload.* Harvard Business Review. https://hbr.org/2012/02/stop-email-overload-1

Gibbs, S. (2016, March 7). *How did email grow from messages between academics to a global epidemic?* The Guardian. https://www.theguardian.com/technology/2016/mar/07/email-ray-tomlinson-history#:~:text=The%20very%20first%20version%20of

Glei, J. K. (2010, December 1). *8 Ways to control your internet addiction.* Business Class: Trends and Insights | American Express. https://www.americanexpress.com/en-us/business/trends-and-insights/articles/8-ways-to-control-your-internet-addiction-1/

Glover, S. (2016, September 15). *50 Things to do without technology.* MetroKids. https://www.metrokids.com/50-things-to-do-without-technology/

Gregory, C. (2016). *Internet addiction disorder - Signs, symptoms, and treatments.* Psycom.net - Mental Health Treatment Resource since 1986. https://www.psycom.net/iadcriteria.html#symptoms

Guertler, D., Rumpf, H.-J., Bischof, A., Kastirke, N., Petersen, K. U., John, U., & Meyer, C. (2013). *Assessment of problematic internet use by the compulsive internet use scale and the internet addiction test: A sample of problematic and pathological gamblers.* European Addiction Research, 20(2), 75–81. https://doi.org/10.1159/000355076

Hall, J. (2019, September 24). *How to quit social media for a happier and more focused life.* Lifehack. https://www.lifehack.org/846374/quitting-social-media

Hartney, E. (2019). *What are the official criteria for addiction?* Verywell Mind. https://www.verywellmind.com/what-are-the-official-criteria-for-addiction-22493

Healthline. (2019, October 29). *How to break a habit: 15 Tips for success.* Healthline. https://www.healthline.com/health/how-to-break-a-habit#dont-ignore-progress

Healthy Options. (2019). *Social media addiction: Causes and Cures.* Healthy Options. https://www.healthyoptions.com.ph/newsdigest/beautiful-and-healthy-bones/social-media-addiction-causes-and-cures

Higgins, M. (2021, September 14). *Do you know how much time you spend online?* NordVPN.com. https://nordvpn.com/blog/lifetime-online-results/#:~:text=The%20average%20internet%20user%20in

Hoeg, N. (2019a). *5 types of internet addiction.* AddictionCenter. https://www.addictioncenter.com/drugs/internet-addiction/

Hoeg, N. (2019b). *Internet addiction.* AddictionCenter. https://www.addictioncenter.com/drugs/internet-addiction/

Ho, L. (2018, March 5). *Powerful daily routine examples for a healthy and high-achieving you.* Lifehack. https://www.lifehack.org/677367/powerful-daily-routine

How to stop internet addiction (with pictures). (2021, October 10). In wikiHow. https://www.wikihow.com/Stop-Internet-Addiction

Islamie Farsani, S., Allahbakhshi, K., Valipour, A. A., & Mohammadian-Hafshejani, A. (2016). *Some facts on problematic internet use and sleep disturbance among adolescents.* Iranian Journal of Public Health, 45(11), 1531–1532. https://www.ncbi.nlm.nih.gov/pmc/articles/PMC5182270/#:~:text=Internet%20addiction%20and%20other%20problematic

Jonas, N. (2022, May 12). *8 Ways to set boundaries with social media if it's affecting your mental health.* Www.glamour.co.za. https://www.glamour.co.za/wellness/mindfulness/8-ways-to-set-boundaries-with-social-media-if-its-affecting-your-mental-health-340aab16-ff1e-4d74-89ca-89456974e23f

Jones, G. (2018, January 31). *7 Simple steps to a digital detox.* Www.nea.org. https://www.nea.org/advocating-for-change/new-from-nea/7-simple-steps-digital-detox

Jones, H. (2019, November 27). *Is time blocking effective?* Calendar. https://www.calendar.com/blog/is-time-blocking-effective/

Jones, L. (2021, November 8). *How to manage email overload at work.* Www.flowrite.com. https://www.flowrite.com/blog/email-overload

Koetsier, J. (2020, February 28). *There are now 8.9 million mobile apps, and China is 40% of mobile app spending.* Forbes. https://www.forbes.com/sites/johnkoetsier/2020/02/28/there-are-now-89-million-mobile-apps-and-china-is-40-of-mobile-app-spending/?sh=5a00ba3121dd

Komar, M. (2016, January 25). *7 Tips on how to actually stay on schedule, once & for all.* Bustle. https://www.bustle.com/articles/137582-7-tips-on-how-to-actually-stay-on-schedule-once-for-all

Lai, I. H., Kim, D., & Jeong, E. J. (2016). *Online digital game addiction: How does social relationship impact game addiction.* AMCIS 2016 Proceedings. https://aisel.aisnet.org/amcis2016/HCI/Presentations/10/

Lau, G. (n.d.). *How to manage email overload: Tips for inbox zero.* Dialpad. https://www.dialpad.com/blog/email-overload/#:~:text=Simply%20put%2C%20email%20overload%20is

Lee, J. (2016, February 4). *5 Ways technology might be feeding your depression.* MakeUseOf. https://www.makeuseof.com/tag/5-ways-technology-might-be-feeding-depression/

Longstreet, P., & Brooks, S. (2017). Life satisfaction: A key to managing internet & social media addiction. Technology in Society, 50, 73–77. https://doi.org/10.1016/j.techsoc.2017.05.003

MacKay, J. (2018, August 2). *10 Email canned responses that will save you hours every week.* RescueTime Blog. https://blog.rescuetime.com/canned-responses-gmail/

MacKay, J. (2019, December 16). *50 Inspirational (And actionable) Time management quotes.* RescueTime Blog. https://blog.rescuetime.com/time-management-quotes/

Manor Clinic. (2021). *Internet addiction signs* | Symptoms of internet addiction. Www.themanorclinic.com. https://www.themanorclinic.com/addiction-treatment/internet-addiction-help/internet-addiction-symptoms

MasterClass. (2022, April 5). *How to make a schedule: 6 tips for scheduling.* MasterClass. https://www.masterclass.com/articles/how-to-make-a-schedule

Meerkerk, G.-J., van den Eijnden, R. J. M., Vermulst, A. A., & Garretsen, H. (2009, February). *The compulsive internet use scale (CIUS): Some psychometric properties.* Research Gate. https://www.researchgate.net/publication/23652985_The_Compulsive_Internet_Use_Scale_CIUS_Some_psychometric_properties

Merriam-Webster. (1847a). *Addiction.* In Merriam-Webster. Encyclopedia Britannica Inc. https://www.merriam-webster.com/dictionary/addiction

Merriam-Webster. (1847b). *Detox.* In Merriam-Webster. Encyclopedia Britannica. https://www.merriam-webster.com/dictionary/detox

Merriam-Webster. (1847c). *Schedule.* In Merriam-Webster. Encyclopædia Britannica. https://www.merriam-webster.com/dictionary/schedule

Milasauskiene, E., Burkauskas, J., Podlipskyte, A., Király, O., Demetrovics, Z., Ambrasas, L., & Steibliene, V. (2021, August 26). *Compulsive internet use scale: Psychometric properties and associations with sleeping patterns, mental health, and well-being in lithuanian medical students during the coronavirus disease 2019 pandemic.* Frontiers. https://www.frontiersin.org/articles/10.3389/fpsyg.2021.685137/full#:~:text=The%20Compulsive%20Internet%20Use%20Scale%20(CIUS)%20has%20been%20proposed%20as,measuring%20PIU%20at%20the%20time.

Miller, A. (2019, December 9). *25 Benefits of creating a schedule for your tasks.* Calendar. https://www.calendar.com/blog/25-benefits-of-creating-a-schedule-for-your-tasks/

Miller, C. (2022, April 14). *Does social media cause depression?* Child Mind Institute. https://childmind.org/article/is-social-media-use-causing-depression/#:~:text=Some%20experts%20see%20the%20rise

Oasis Recovery Runcorn. (n.d.). *14 Signs and symptoms of internet addiction.* Oasis Rehab. https://www.oasisrehab.co.uk/internet-addiction/

PA Families Inc. (n.d.). *Risk factors and addictive behavior.* Pafamiliesinc.org. http://pafamiliesinc.org/understanding-systems/drugs-alcohol/risk-factors

Pettersen, H., Landheim, A., Skeie, I., Biong, S., Brodahl, M., Oute, J., & Davidson, L. (2019). *How Social Relationships Influence Substance Use Disorder Recovery: A Collaborative Narrative Study.* Substance Abuse: Research and Treatment, 13, 117822181983337. https://doi.org/10.1177/1178221819833379

Primrose Lodge. (n.d.). *Internet addiction: Signs, symptoms and treatment.* Primrose Lodge. https://www.primroselodge.com/behavioural-addictions/internet/

Quiñones-García, C., & Korak-Kakabadse, N. (2014). *Compulsive internet use in adults: A study of prevalence and drivers within the current economic climate in the UK.* Computers in Human Behavior, 30, 171–180. https://doi.org/10.1016/j.chb.2013.08.004

Reed, M. (2017, February 21). *How internet addiction is harming your brain, your health, and your sleep.* Healthcentral.com; HealthCentral. https://www.healthcentral.com/article/how-internet-addiction-is-harming-your-brain-your-health-and-your-sleep

Rennolds, N. (2021, January 11). *How to quit social media for good.* MUO. https://www.makeuseof.com/how-to-quit-social-media/

reSTART, T. (2009, September 7). *Compulsive Internet Use Scale (CIUS).* ReSTART. https://www.netaddictionrecovery.com/compulsive-internet-use-scale-cius/

Ring Central. (2020, April 15). *9 strategies, tips, and tools to stop email overload in its tracks.* RingCentral. https://www.ringcentral.com/us/en/blog/email-overload/

Robinson, L., & Smith, M. (2020, January 16). *Social media and mental health.* Https://Www.helpguide.org. https://www.helpguide.org/articles/mental-health/social-media-and-mental-health.htm#:~:text=The%20negative%20aspects%20of%20social%20media&text=However%2C%20multiple%20studies%20have%20found

Sherry, K. (2020, November 19). *The benefits of doing a digital detox.* Verywell Mind. https://www.verywellmind.com/why-and-how-to-do-a-digital-detox-4771321#toc-how-to-do-a-digital-detox

Singh, J. (2016, October). *Internet addiction and social isolation.* Research Gate. https://www.researchgate.net/publication/308927635_Internet_addiction_and_social_isolation

Šmotek, M., Fárková, E., Manková, D., & Kopřivová, J. (2020). *Evening and night exposure to screens of media devices and its association with subjectively perceived sleep: Should "light hygiene" be given more attention?.* Sleep Health, 6(4), 498–505. https://doi.org/10.1016/j.sleh.2019.11.007

Sparks, C. (2021, May 25). *Triggers — The key to building and breaking habits.* Medium. https://medium.com/@ForcingFunction/triggers-the-key-to-building-and-breaking-habits-fa8ed153ab0c#:~:text=As%20the%20%5Btrigger%5D

Sreenivas, S. (2021, May 12). *Digital detox: What to know.* WebMD. https://www.webmd.com/balance/what-is-digital-detox

Stathopoulos, C. (2022, April 17). *How to do a digital detox.* WikiHow. https://www.wikihow.com/Do-a-Digital-Detox

Statista. (2022, April 4). *U.S. social users who considered leaving select social networks 2020.* Statista; S. Dixon. https://www.statista.com/statistics/262145/us-social-networkers-who-want-use-social-networking-less/#:~:text=Overall%2C%2045%20percent%20of%20Facebook

Studios Guys. (n.d.). *12 Examples of automation in Real Life.* Studious Guy. https://studiousguy.com/automation-examples/

The Economic Times. (2018, January 14). *Here's how technology affects our life - Technology addiction.* The Economic Times. https://economictimes.indiatimes.

com/tech/internet/heres-how-technology-affects-our-life/technology-addiction/
slideshow/62497145.cms

Thomas, M. (2018, June 5). *Email overload? Here's why you're drowning – And how to fix It*. Maura Thomas. https://maurathomas.com/drowning-in-email-overload/

Time management: Creating and using a schedule creating a schedule. (n.d.). https://www.marquette.edu/counseling/documents/TimeManagementandProcrastinationHandout.pdf

Tulane University. (2020, December 8). *Understanding the effects of social isolation on mental health.* Publichealth.tulane.edu; Tulane University. https://publichealth.tulane.edu/blog/effects-of-social-isolation-on-mental-health/

Turning Point of Tampa. (2019, October 3). *Environmental risk factors & their role in drug addiction.* Turning Point of Tampa. https://www.tpoftampa.com/environmental-factors-and-their-role-in-addiction/#:~:text=A%20person

Weber, M. (2019, May 22). *Understanding addiction.* HelpGuide.org. https://www.helpguide.org/harvard/how-addiction-hijacks-the-brain.htm

WebMD. (2021, April 22). *Understanding the Basics of Depression.* WebMD. https://www.webmd.com/depression/understanding-depression-basics#:~:text=Researchers%20say%20that%20their%20work

Webroot. (2017). Webroot.com. https://www.webroot.com/za/en/resources/tips-articles/internet-addiction-too-much-time-online

Wilber, J. (2022 21). *The internet and social Isolation: Does correlation indicate causation?* Owlcation - Education. https://owlcation.com/social-sciences/The-Internet-and-Social-Isolation-Causation-or-Correlation

Worlddata.info. (2021). *Average life expectancy by country.* Worlddata.info. https://www.worlddata.info/life-expectancy.php#:~:text=Life%20expectancy%20for%20men%20and%20women&text=The%20world%20average%20age%20of

Young, K. S. (2015, October 6). *What makes the internet addictive: Potential explanations for pathological internet use.* Www.healthyplace.com. https://www.healthyplace.com/addictions/center-for-internet-addiction-recovery/what-makes-the-internet-addictive-potencial

Youshaei, J. (2014, August 1). *Email rehab: 8 Ways to detox from your inbox.* Forbes. https://www.forbes.com/sites/jonyoushaei/2014/08/01/email-rehab/?sh=2a4331a17880

Zuckerman, A. (2020, May 29). *109 Technology addiction statistics: 2020/2021* Data, facts & insights. Compare Camp. https://comparecamp.com/technology-addiction-statistics/#:~:text=According%20to%20a%20study%20in,internet%20and%20social%20media%20worldwide.

Printed in Great Britain
by Amazon

28594210R00076